Mediation and Strategic Change

Lessons from Mediating a Nationwide Doctors' Strike

Moti Mordehai Mironi

Hamilton Books
A member of
The Rowman & Littlefield Publishing Group
Lanham • Boulder • New York • Toronto • Plymouth, UK

Copyright © 2008 by
Hamilton Books
4501 Forbes Boulevard
Suite 200
Lanham, Maryland 20706
Hamilton Books Acquisitions Department (301) 459-3366

Estover Road
Plymouth PL6 7PY
United Kingdom

Library of Congress Control Number: 2008920632
ISBN-13: 978-0-7618-4014-5 (clothbound : alk. paper)
ISBN-10: 0-7618-4014-1 (clothbound : alk. paper)
ISBN-13: 978-0-7618-3987-3 (paperback : alk. paper)
ISBN-10: 0-7618-3987-9 (paperback : alk. paper)
eISBN-13: 978-0-7618-4163-0
eISBN-10: 0-7618-4163-6

Contents

Preface

On the morning of May 27th 2000, as Israel's nationwide doctors' strike was entering its eleventh week, I received a call from the office of the Prime Minister. The Cabinet Secretary was on the line. He was calling on behalf of the Prime Minister. He had a surprising message: (a) the Government had asked the parties to enter mediation; (b) the Prime Minister wanted me to be the mediator; (c) the parties were willing to consider mediation, and had accepted me as the mediator; (d) a well-known businessman whom I had never previously met had been asked to serve as co-mediator; and (e) due to the urgency of the situation, the first mediation session was scheduled for later that day, a mere two hours after my co-mediator was due to return from an overseas business trip.

This call marked the beginning of a six-week, totally consuming mediation marathon and the most intense and complex ADR experience of my life. It ended in an agreement, one which not only settled the strike but also had the potential to transform labor-management relations and human resource management in the medical profession in Israel.

The seeds of the idea to write a case study about the doctors' mediation were planted very shortly after the mediation itself ended. I was asked to present the case at the 7th World Congress of the International Society for Labor Law and Social Security, which was held in September 2000 in Jerusalem. As I was preparing my notes, I was intrigued by the richness and drama of the story, as well as by the insights and lessons that could be learned from our experience. Being both an academic and a practitioner, I felt we should not allow this precious story and insights from it to fade away. There was no one else to undertake such a project.

After the Congress, I was surprised to receive calls from practitioners and scholars from around the world. They had either attended the Congress or had heard about the presentation and wanted to learn more about the doctors' mediation. They were interested in drawing on our experience as they themselves struggled with similar public policy disputes or strikes in essential services.

These messages convinced me to write the story of the doctors' mediation. I received the parties' permission, promising to provide them with a draft for their review before publication. I gathered my notes and went into the woods of Maine to reflect and write this case study.

The more I delved into the case, the more it dawned on me that the story of the doctors' mediation is not just a great story about the value and immense potential of ADR in general and mediation in particular. Nor is it merely an intricate story of the dynamics and complexities of negotiating a multi-party, multi-issue public policy dispute, or a multifaceted story of labor and employment relations or public-sector collective bargaining, or even an insightful illustration of the present crisis in Israel's public health care system. It is a story where several academic disciplines and professional fields intersect and converge: negotiation, ADR, industrial relations, health care, government, communications, law and economics.

Acknowledgments

I would like to thank my friends Chagit and Roger Deitz, who persuaded me to come to Maine, where I wrote this monograph in their inspirational lake-front house on Coffee Pond, a place as tranquil as our mediation was contentious. Roger Deitz, who is also a mediation colleague, deserves special thanks for his valuable contribution in reading and editing earlier drafts.

Mr. Yuval Rachlevski, the Director of Wage and Labor Agreements Division at the Finance Ministry, Dr. Yoram Blashar, Chairman of the Israel Medical Association and Ms. Lea Vapner, Legal Counsel and General Manager of the Israel Medical Association, deserve gratitude for letting me publish the story and for their helpful comments as well.

This is also a great opportunity to thank my partner in the mediation, Miki Federman, our assistant mediators, Jonathan Kowarsky and Gershon Rudich, and our spokesperson, Pnina Elazar, for their outstanding work and their friendship. All the participants in the mediation deserve our gratitude for their commitment and for placing their trust in the mediation process and in us as mediators.

I owe special thanks to Thomas Kochan, David Matz, Robert McKersie and Larry Susskind who read and critiqued an early draft of the manuscript, and provided comments and suggestions that enriched and sharpened the final product. I wish to thank the participants in the Research Seminar of the MIT Institute for Work and Employment, including Marian Baird, Susan Eaton, Russell Lansbury, Nancy Peace and Arnold Zack, for their invaluable thoughts and ideas. Although I am indebted to all those who provided criticisms, comments and questions and see them as important contributors to the final product, the responsibility for it is solely mine. Finally, thanks to my editor, Dr. Adam Vital and to my research assistant, Irena Nutenko for her superb work in compiling the index.

Last but not least, I would like to thank my partner Yael and my children Roy, Hila and Aya, as well as the partners and staff of my law firm, who put up with my being present but absent for the six weeks of the mediation, and who gave me tremendous support and encouragement.

Moti Mironi
Casco, Maine

Introduction

Israel's economic infrastructure and institutions are rooted in traditions that cherish the right to join a union, to bargain collectively and to strike. In this environment, it is not surprising that almost all doctors employed by hospitals and clinics in Israel are unionized.

The doctors are represented by a single union, the Israel Medical Association ("IMA"). Doctors' salaries and other working conditions are set through a nationwide collective bargaining agreement, negotiated primarily with the two largest employers: the state, which operates 21 hospitals and 12 mental health centers, and "Clalit" General Health Services ("Clalit"), which owns and manages 16 hospitals and 206 HMO-type clinics.

In March 2000 the IMA called a strike of all doctors in all hospital and HMO-type clinics. Since private medical care serves only a small fraction of the nation, the strike had a devastating impact on the public at large. By May 27th the doctors had been on strike for more than ten weeks. Suffering was mounting, and the public outcry was growing; political pressure on the Government to end the strike reached new heights.

That morning I received a telephone call from the Prime Minister's office. The Cabinet Secretary was on the line. He was calling on behalf of the Prime Minister. He had a surprising message to convey: (a) the Government had asked the parties to enter mediation; (b) the Prime Minister wanted me to be the mediator; and (c) the parties were willing to consider mediation and had accepted me as the mediator.

The Prime Minister's initiative came as a surprise. Unlike the United States, Canada, and certain other Western countries, Israel has no tradition of third-party involvement in labor disputes, neither in the form of mediation nor of arbitration.[1] Moreover, this was not an ordinary dispute. The stakes were high. There was enormous pressure on the Government to intervene, either by ordering the Finance Minister to accept the doctors' demands or by invoking emergency regulations to compel the doctors to return to work.[2]

The Prime Minister's invitation to me personally was also unexpected. True, I had considerable academic experience in labor law and labor relations and substantial practical experience in dispute resolution as a mediator and arbitrator, but I had never held public office and was not associated with the public service.[3]

I accepted the Cabinet Secretary's invitation. He then made two additional disclosures. First, another person had been asked to serve as co-mediator. Although his name was familiar to me, we had never met. In addition, he was not a professional mediator. Second, because of the urgency of the situation, the first meeting was already scheduled for later the same day, two hours after my co-mediator was due to return from an overseas business trip.

The strike had already entered its tenth week; I believed that my assignment would most likely be short-lived—a classic crisis mediation.[4] But, in the event, it turned out to be neither short nor crisis-type mediation. The doctors' mediation was a six-week marathon, a totally consuming process—the most intense and complex ADR experience of my life. It ended in a strategic agreement, one which not only settled the strike but also had the potential to transform the terrain of labor-management and employment relations in Israel's health care industry.

This book tells the story of the doctors' mediation as seen through my eyes as the leader of the mediation team. It is only natural to expect each participant to have his or her own personal perspective and to draw different conclusions from our one common experience. The purpose of this study is to provide insight that will, hopefully, help future disputants, lawyers, advisors, negotiators, mediators, ADR practitioners and researchers.

The rich and colorful details of the doctors' strike and the mediation that ended it are a compelling story, and they are described here. As events unfold, a brief description of the participants, the dispute, and the background will be offered to help set the stage and the tone of this extraordinary mediation story.

The reader will not find a detailed account of every day of the mediation. Only highlights will be presented whose purpose is to enable the reader to locate the lessons and insights in their context.

NOTES

1. Ruth Ben Israel & Mordehai Mironi, "The Role of Neutrals in the Resolution of Interest Disputes–Israel" 10 *Comparative Lab. L. J.* 356, 360 (1989).

2. Under Article 9 of the Law and Administration Ordinance, 1948, when Parliament has declared a state of emergency, the government may authorize the Prime Minister or any other minister to issue emergency regulations in the interests of the defense of the state, public security and the maintenance of supplies and essential services. A state of emergency was declared in 1948 and it is still in force. Furthermore, all ministers have been authorized by the government to issue emergency regulations. Thus they would not need specific authorization to act. The emergency regulations usually authorize government officers or managers in both public and private undertakings to issue specific back-to-work orders on an ad hoc basis, under which particular employees or groups of employees are temporarily denied the freedom to strike. Mordehai Mironi, 'Back to Work Emergency Orders; Government Intervention in Labor Disputes in Essential Services" 15 *Hebrew U. L. Rev.* 350 (1986).

3. The press emphasized that I was also the President of the Israel Mediation Association.

4. For the distinction between crisis mediation and preventive or strategic mediation see: Thomas A. Kochan & John Cutcher-Gershenfeld, *Final Report on the National Performance Review Survey for the Federal Mediation and Conciliation Service* 22 (1997).

Chapter One

The Landscape

To begin, one must appreciate the unique history and the present state of industrial relations in Israel in general and of the Israeli public health care system and the medical profession in particular. It is necessary to identify the major actors and understand their intricate relationships.

Israel has been described as a "labor state"—a state run by a labor movement.[1] At one time, the rate of unionization was as high as 85%. One union represented practically every unionized worker in Israel. This union was the Histadrut. It was founded in 1920, twenty-eight years before the State of Israel. It functioned as a government in anticipation of a government, and amassed enormous economic and political power and influence.

Like other professionals, doctors are highly unionized. More than 90% are union members. In contrast to almost all other white-collar employees who are represented by the Histadrut, doctors and certain other professionals, such as journalists, high school teachers and university professors, belong to their own union. In the case of doctors, they are represented by the IMA, which is independent of the Histadrut and which represents 16,000 doctors.

The IMA was founded in 1912, thirty-six years before the State of Israel. By its philosophy and function the IMA does not limit itself to trade unionism. It also serves as a professional organization, providing a broad array of services, including licensing, insurance and educational functions, as well as being a self-governing professional organization in terms of ethics and discipline. The IMA has also been involved in public health matters and in projects of national importance, such as the absorption of the thousands of doctors who immigrated to Israel from the former Soviet Republic.

The IMA's constituency is highly heterogeneous. It represents many members with different and sometimes conflicting interests. First, the IMA is a

federation of two unions: the Association of State Doctors and the Association of the General Health Services Doctors. The latter represents two distinct
populations—doctors who work in hospitals and doctors who work in clinics.
Second, the IMA negotiates on behalf of doctors who work under a variety of
conditions. Third, in contrast to the worldwide phenomenon where senior
management is either not unionized or has a separate union, the IMA represents all levels of doctors within a single union, from interns to general managers of hospitals. Fourth, IMA members are divided into fifty-one occupa-
tional groups, some of which have been on the rise in terms of both their
status and the volume of their work, while the importance of others has been
on the decline. Finally, the IMA has always negotiated nationwide collective
agreements. Yet there is a clear division between the doctors who work in the
large metropolitan areas such as Tel-Aviv and Jerusalem and those practicing
elsewhere in the country.

Even before the enactment of the National Health Law of 1995, medical
care in Israel was predominantly public and semi-public. This phenomenon
can be attributed to the ideology of the founders of the state. They believed
in building a new society premised on principles of social justice and mutual
aid. The idea was led by the Histadrut, which never saw itself as a traditional
trade union. It has historically been party to all economic and social welfare
initiatives of national concern. The jewel in the crown of the Histadrut's economic and mutual aid activities has always been the provision of health care
through Clalit.

Although private medicine has expanded in recent years, it serves only a
small fraction of the population. Medicine is dominated by two large employers: the Histadrut-affiliated provider, Clalit, and the state. Clalit is the primary provider of health care to more than half of Israel's population. It owns
and runs 16 hospitals and 206 HMO clinics, and employs two-thirds of the
16,000 members of the IMA.

The state runs 21 hospitals. In addition, there are several hospitals that are
owned by the municipalities of Tel Aviv and Haifa and by non-profit associations, such as Hadassah, which operates two research hospitals affiliated
with the Hebrew University, and Sha'arei Tzedek in Jerusalem, as well as
several hundreds clinics run by two other medium-size, semi-public HMO-
type providers of medical services.

The three large employers that operate hospitals, i.e., Clalit, the state and
Hadassah, differ not only in their respective size and their facilities; their
doctors enjoy different working conditions. For example, Clalit's doctors
have a contributory pension, while state-employed doctors have a budgetary, non-contributory pension. And, unlike the state's and Clalit's doctors,
only Hadassah doctors enjoy extra benefits, such as sabbatical years and

special funds for scientific exchange that are usually enjoyed by university faculty members.

Doctors' salaries and working conditions are governed by a nationwide multi-employer collective agreement, which is referred to in the case law as a "pluralistic special collective agreement." Traditionally, it is signed by the IMA on the one hand and the three major employers (Clalit, the state and Hadassah) on the other. The other employers in the industry usually follow this nationwide agreement as "units of direct impact".[2]

Admittedly, the landscape is complicated. But there is more. The chief negotiator representing the employers is the Director of Wage and Labor Agreements Division (hereby the "Director" or the "Director of the Wage and Labor Agreements Division"), a division of the Finance Ministry that administers and enforces the wage control program. The Wage and Labor Agreements Division (hereby the "Division" or the "Wage and Labor Agreements Division") employs professionals, primarily economists and lawyers. Since 1985 the public sector in Israel has been under a strict regime of wage control. The public sector is defined broadly, and includes the civil service, local government, state agencies, government corporations, universities, and every other organization or institution that receives government funding. Needless to say, all employers in the health care sector (with few exceptions) fall under the Director's jurisdiction.

Under Israeli law, employers in the public sector are not allowed to increase wages or benefits to employees either collectively or individually without the consent of the Director of the Wage and Labor Agreements Division. Practically speaking, the staff of the Wage and Labor Agreements Division often acts as chief negotiator, and the division's Director himself leads principal contract negotiations. Given the fact that the state is the second largest health care employer and that all major organizations that employ doctors are funded by the state, the Director of the Wage and Labor Agreements Division has a lead role in contract negotiations.

NOTES

1. Nadav Safran, *The United States and Israel* 84 (1963).
2. Arnold R. Weber, "Stability and Change in the Structure of Collective Bargaining" in *Challenges to Collective Bargaining*, Lloyd Ulman Ed. 13, 14 (1967).

Chapter Two

Entry into the Mediation

My co-mediator and I had no time to prepare. We certainly had no time to plan. Several hours after the Cabinet Secretary's call, we convened a pre-mediation meeting at the Accadia Hotel in Herzliya. There I met for the first time both my co-mediator and the parties' representatives.[1] It was also my introduction to the dispute. Press accounts had provided little insight into the underlying interests.

Walking into the room, I saw that two of the eight present were representatives of the Prime Minister—the Government Secretary and the Prime Minister's special advisor on the doctors' strike. For better or for worse, this mediation was going to be conducted with the Prime Minister at the table. As the mediation progressed, it became clear that in addition to the Prime Minister, several Cabinet members, notably the Finance Minister and the Minister of Health, were going to play pivotal roles.

The participants had only a brief opportunity to become acquainted. I opened with an in-depth explanation of mediation. Special emphasis was given to three aspects: (a) that total power resides with the parties; (b) that the mediators' role is facilitative only; and (c) that mediation has the potential for creating value.

The time was well spent, since only the Director of the Wage and Labor Agreements Division and I had prior mediation experience. I felt that sharing a common expectation of the process was critical to guaranteeing that all sides would make an informed decision to commit to mediation, instead of merely fulfilling the Prime Minster's request without actually knowing what mediation was.

We asked the parties to describe the conflict, its main issues, the composition of the parties, the status of the strike and of negotiations, and to list issues that were no longer in dispute.

The picture was astonishing. The parties' leaders appeared to be skilful and experienced professionals with a history of mutual respect. We learned that they had been negotiating for over two years, the previous four-year agreement having expired in June 1998. During all that time and despite intensive effort, the parties had been unable to reach agreement on even a single issue!

I thought it was very important for the leaders to reach agreement on something as soon as possible. To this end, I devoted significant effort to facilitating negotiations over initial ground rules for the mediation. Later on I would be able to remind the parties that they had been successful in establishing mediation ground rules by mutual consent. These were very important examples that helped them reach agreement on substantive issues in the later stages of the process. Therefore, the rest of the first session was in fact spent formulating the mediation ground rules. Given the history of negotiations and the immense pressures, even organizing the mediation proved to be a difficult task.

The thorniest issue was the Government's request that the doctors discontinue the strike while mediation was in progress. In Israel, the Government traditionally does not negotiate with workers who are striking. The request was vehemently rejected by the IMA. Nevertheless the Government agreed to stay at the table. At this point we had a commitment to the mediation.

It took us three hours to agree on the following mediation ground rules:

(1) The mediation was to conclude within two, or at most three weeks.
(2) For this limited period of time, the status quo would be maintained, i.e., there would be no escalation of the strike. This compromise was possible, as doctors' strikes are rarely full strikes; this strike was no exception. The IMA had not actually taken the extreme step of calling for a total walkout. Instead, it engaged in a partial strike, in which once a week the doctors worked with a skeleton crew on a rotating basis and in various locations. In addition, they performed only life-saving operations, and severely curtailed services in out-patient clinics. At the time we began our mediation, the strike was about to escalate; the IMA was threatening a total walkout, which would have left only skeleton crews at hospitals to deal with extreme emergencies.
(3) Due to the urgency of the situation and the self-imposed deadline, the parties and the mediators would meet daily without time limits.
(4) At the IMA's request, the Division would supply the IMA with data regarding doctors' earnings and benefits.
(5) The mediation would be held at neutral sites where several joint meetings and private caucuses could take place simultaneously. Prior to the mediation, all negotiations had been held alternately at the offices of the IMA or at the offices of the Wage and Labor Agreements Division. The parties

accepted the mediators' suggestion that the change of location signified a
new era in the negotiations.

With these agreements in hand, we were ready to break for a long weekend. We had set the stage, and would reconvene the following week with the
full negotiation teams for the first substantive mediation sessions.

NOTES

1. The employers were represented by the Director of the Wage and Labor Agreements Division, Mr. Yuval Rachlevski, and the Associate Director Mr. Yossi Cohen.
The IMA was represented by its Chairman, Dr. Yoram Blashar, and its General Manager, and in-house counsel Ms. Leah Vapner, while the Prime Minister's representatives were the Cabinet Secretary, Mr. Itzhak Herzog, and one of the Prime Minister's
personal advisors, Prof. Amiram Carmon. With the exception of the Director of the
Wage and Labor Agreements Division, I had not met any of them before.

Chapter Three

Putting the Act Together

In retrospect, the long weekend was critical for the success of the mediation. My co-mediator and I badly needed time to get acquainted, to set our own mediation house in order, and to address logistical issues. We had to build a mediation team, identify underlying issues, and decide on locations for future meetings.

BUILDING THE MEDIATION TEAM

During the organizational session I only had the chance to exchange a few sentences with my co-mediator. He told me that he had never been part of a mediation process before and was not familiar with the theory or practice of dispute resolution. Consequently, he wanted me to take the lead, promising to be a good student. When the organizational session was over, we realized that we definitely needed to deepen our acquaintance and to learn how best to work together. After all, co-mediation requires that the two mediators play the music of mediation together in harmony.

The next day we met for several hours at his office. I concluded that I could not have had a better partner. Not only did we connect on a personal level, we immediately found we could work together. Our backgrounds made us a synergetic team.

Michael (Miki) Federman, the co-mediator, is a well-known businessman. His family owns the Dan Hotels, a leading chain with hotels located throughout Israel, and has interests in major high-tech industrial and commercial undertakings. He holds a degree in economics. Over the years, as the Chair of the Labor Committee of the Association of Hotel Owners and as an industrialist, he established close ties with the professional staff at the Finance

Minister's office. In addition, he had extensive practical experience in labor relations. Although he had neither training nor experience in mediation, he possessed the right personality: sensitivity, patience, warmth, ability to listen, openness and integrity. Finally, he was also a close friend of the Prime Minister.

Following the good advice given by a former colleague,[1] we added two assistant mediators to our team, Jonathan Kowarsky and Gershon Rudich. Both are mediators. The former was selected primarily because of his mediation expertise, the latter because of his proficiency in economics and data analysis. On the basis of what was said during the organizational session, we expected difficult discussions and sharp disagreements regarding the provision of data and methodology in analyzing the economic implications of possible proposals. Once the mediation began in earnest, it soon became clear that adding assistant mediators to the mediation team had been a wise decision.

PLANNING

Since we had not yet met the full delegations and had little information about the dispute, we concentrated at this stage on two aspects: organization and the media.

The Participants

In a multi-party high-profile public dispute such as the doctors' strike, it was only to be expected that many people would want a place at the table. This was partly because everybody who was likely to be affected by the outcome needed to be part of the decision-making process. But to make progress we knew we had to meet in small (and sometimes extremely small) groups. These meetings might cause problems with those left out. There is always the risk that the price for having been left out will be exacted at a crucial moment when the support of those who were excluded is critical.

Furthermore, we assumed that at least on the Government's side there were high-ranking officials who would insist on participating but who would be unable or unwilling to attend every session. We thought this might present a problem, since mediation is often a transforming experience. It was important that all participants in the resolution of the strike be exposed to the process of transformation. It turned out that most members of the employers' team lived and worked in Jerusalem, while most of the IMA's representatives lived and worked in the Tel Aviv metropolitan area. (The drive from Tel Aviv to Jerusalem takes about an hour and a half.) Although we lived in Tel Aviv, we were willing to suggest that sessions be conducted alternately in Jerusalem and Tel Aviv, as one of the mediation team's contributions.

We decided to raise these two issues at the next session, and to try to come up with solutions that would be incorporated into the parties' ground rules.

The Media

The doctors' strike was big news, and had been so since the strike began. For the mediation to be successful it had to be conducted under conditions of strict confidentiality. We needed to find a way to differentiate, for purposes of media coverage, between the strike itself and its mediation. One way to do so was to effect a media blackout of the mediation. We knew that this was an unrealistic expectation, especially in Israel. We therefore suggested adding a professional spokesperson to the mediation team. This person would issue joint statements, keep the media off the premises where negotiations were being conducted, and help us monitor the parties' compliance with the ground rules as they related to the media.

Miki suggested Pnina Elazar. She had formerly worked in public relations for the IMA and knew the industry well. The employers were advised of her previous relationship with the IMA and did not see a problem.

In retrospect, it is hard to overstate the importance of hiring Pnina or her contribution to the success of the mediation.

THE LOCATION

Here again, Miki Federman proved resourceful and helpful. He suggested that the sessions be held at his family's hotels. His personal involvement in the mediation assured that we enjoyed affordable rates, first-rate service and priority in access to conference rooms. The ability to use the hotels for mediation sessions and the endless willingness of the staff to help with all our needs, day and night, relieved us all of a huge logistic responsibility.

NOTES

1. Professor David Matz.

Chapter Four

The Opening Session

The first thing I noticed when I walked into the hotel where the first session was to be held was that the lobby and the conference room were filled with reporters and television crews. Our spokesperson was already there, advising the media to take pictures and conduct interviews since they were not likely to see the mediation room or to be able to speak with the parties or the mediators until the mediation was over. The media was ushered out after the first sentences of my opening remarks. Thanks to Pnina's superb performance, we did not see reporters again until the ceremonial press conference at which the agreement was signed.

Twenty-nine people were at the table, including the four-member mediation team and our spokesperson. The IMA was represented by twelve people: its Chairman, in-house counsel and General Manager, three vice-chairmen (the chairmen of the doctors' associations of state hospitals, Clalit hospitals and Clalit clinics), one union official from the Clalit clinics, three union officials from the state and Clalit hospitals, the IMA's outside accountant, and two members of the IMA staff.

The employers were represented by eleven people. The Finance Ministry was represented by the Director of the Wage and Labor Agreements Division, his associate, and an analyst, all of whom were from the Wage and Labor Agreements Division, and by two officials from the Division of Budget. The Ministry of Health was represented by its General Manager and the Officer of Manpower. The Civil Service Commission and Clalit each had two representatives. Hadassah was represented by its Human Resources manager. Finally, there was the Cabinet Secretary.

In passing, I should note that if the number of participants seemed unwieldy at the time, later in the mediation it would grow by more than twenty-five percent once the lawyers were brought in!

We started the session with a standard mediator's opening. We explained how mediation differs from adjudication, arbitration or a committee of experts. We stressed that our role was not to decide right or wrong or to impose a solution. Since the parties had the knowledge, the power and all the responsibility, we were there only to help them reach an amicable solution that would hopefully meet their interests. To achieve this goal, we would encourage them throughout the process to identify their underlying interests, since these would hold the key to a solution.

We spoke at length about the importance of strict confidentiality, and explained that we might conduct private caucuses and that we might consult with people outside the negotiating teams. We added that, as part of the mediation, all such meetings would be covered by the same rules of confidentiality.

Finally, we underscored the fact that although mediation might initially appear to them as an extension of the preceding two years of negotiations, it was actually a very different process. We asked for the parties' cooperation, trust, patience, commitment, and optimism. With these, we were confident, they would reach an agreement.

After the opening statement, we introduced the mediation team and reminded the participants of the ground rules they had agreed to at the organizational meeting. This was important, as the IMA's officials were concerned that the Government had no intention of reaching a settlement, and they feared that mediation was merely a device to bring the strike to an end just as the Government was beginning to feel the political pressure. The fact that in the organizational meeting we had agreed the mediation would not affect the strike helped to address this concern.

Once the full forum ratified the first set of ground rules, we raised for discussion our proposal concerning the media and the location of the meetings. We stressed that the mediation ground rules could be altered at the parties' consent. We invited their input in process-related issues.

In view of the large number of participants and their seniority, we were primarily interested in sorting out two problems. First, we needed the flexibility to form working groups and the ability to meet with only a few people at a time without offending the rest of the group. Second, we had to avoid the so-called "train station syndrome," i.e., people entering and leaving mediation sessions, which would disrupt the transformation process.

Although we had a full table and tensions were high, the tone was polite and productive. The following understandings were reached:

(1) The parties would not contact the press regarding the mediation; only the spokesperson would speak to the media. All communications would be joint statements of all parties, arrived at by consent. In addition, the parties would direct their own spokespersons to minimize all other reporting

regarding individual doctors or the medical profession. This was added
because the IMA alleged that since the beginning of the strike the Government had been trying to apply pressure on the doctors by releasing sto-
ries about doctors who were under investigation for alleged income tax
irregularities in their private practice.

(2) Within the mediation, a principle of transparency would be observed.
Data and documents would be available to everyone. Private caucusing
would be limited as much as possible.

(3) At the mediators' suggestion, sessions would be held alternately in
Jerusalem and the Tel Aviv area. Whenever possible, sessions would be
scheduled to allow participants to attend to urgent business matters. For
this reason, some sessions started at noon, we often worked late into the
night.

(4) No written record would be kept.

(5) All participants accepted the need to conduct certain sessions of the mediation in small groups.

(6) With the exception of doctors on call, cellular phones would be turned off
during sessions.

(7) First names would be used.

At the end of the session, an IMA leader who had earlier voiced his pessimism about the process told us that the mood was unprecedented. After
hundreds of hours of barren negotiations, he found that parties were capa-
ble of agreeing, and, more importantly, speaking and actually listening to
each other. He was beginning to trust the process and was willing to give
it a chance. When we heard this comment we felt that two years of icy negotiations had begun to thaw. Only at the end of the mediation did we discover how important this leader's transformation was to the success of the
mediation.

Chapter Five

Learning About the Dispute

Once ground rules were established, we asked the parties to present the open issues.

The IMA chairman listed fifteen demands. Among them were: increasing doctors' base salaries by 100%, overhauling the compensation structure in order to avoid the sharp decline in earnings during paid vacation, sick leave and pension (all of which were calculated on the basis of the base salary), abolishing long-term employment of doctors through intermediaries and temporary help agencies (manpower contractors), limiting interns' work hours after on-duty shifts, increasing continuing education allowances,[1] providing for the rotation of departmental heads and heads of units, organizational reform of emergency rooms and the introduction of emergency medicine as a new area of specialization, the organizational restructuring of hospitals by creating divisions and the appointment of division chiefs, and changing staffing and bed allocation criteria in hospital departments where such changes were warranted as a result of radical changes in medical treatment.

The employers' list comprised sixteen demands. Many demands appeared on both lists, although expressed differently. There were several new issues on the employers' list. Among them were: reaching a long-term agreement, transferring state-employed doctors to a contributory pension fund, introducing procedures to assure the presence of doctors at hospitals or clinics during scheduled working hours (in other words, some form of punch clock).

The list of issues brought home still another troubling observation about the preceding negotiations. The four-year collective agreement (whose expiration followed by two years of unresolved contract renewal negotiations had led to the strike and, ultimately, to the mediation), had expired in June 1998. Apparently, the last four issues on the IMA's list[2] were not new; they were part of the 1994

13

agreement, which provided that during the term of the agreement (1994–1998) they would be resolved through a bipartite labor-management committee.[3] Six years later these four issues were still unresolved. Strange as it may sound, the employers had the same interest as the doctors in resolving these long-standing issues. In other words, these were classic "integrative issues."[4] Yet the parties were unable to resolve them even through bipartite committees, and they were still on the table in June 2000.

Throughout the mediation, the list of demands was in a state of flux. Some of the original demands became critical, some turned out to be less important, and some disappeared altogether. At the beginning we kept the combined list of issues in mind, and asked the parties to make a full presentation of one issue at a time. We urged them to explain their concerns from a broad perspective and to concentrate their presentations on how and why a particular issue had become important and to whom, rather than focus on their positions or specific demands.

Expecting the presentations to be long, we asked the twenty-nine representatives to listen and be patient and to overcome the urge to respond out of turn.[5] We explained that in mediation it is vital that everyone be satisfied that his or her point of view has been heard and understood by everyone else. We added that listening quietly to the other party's presentation does not mean that the listener agrees or accepts everything that is said. So as not to put their patience to too harsh a test, we promised to alternate the order of presentations. Finally, we indicated that once the main speaker finished talking, all team members would have the opportunity to add their own views. Although there was a clear sense of urgency, we were convinced that at this stage it would be wrong not to allow everyone in the room to have their say.

We had to invest substantial efforts to convince the participants to internalize these new rules of discourse—rules which not only ran counter to their instincts as combative negotiators but were also completely foreign to Israeli culture.

In our eyes, the start of the mediation also marked the beginning of a parallel seminar[6] in which the mediators and the parties' representatives were playing roles both as teachers and students. As teachers, we constantly taught the participants about the mediation process and how to enhance their ability to utilize the mediation, especially by carefully listening to each other. When we placed ourselves in the students' seats it was not only to learn, but also because we believed that people deepen their own understanding of, and their insight into, their needs and interests by teaching others about them.

During the seminar, we kept asking the parties to explore their underlying goals, assumptions, concerns, constraints and priorities. We also asked them to clarify and to define the concepts they were using.

In this parallel seminar the mediators were introduced to the health care industry, its economics, institutional structure, management, principal players and history. At the same time, each side enhanced its understanding of the issues, and of the other side's perception of them.

While we were learning about the dispute, the parties were being informed about mediation. One incident that took place during that first week demonstrated the virtue of mediation and its potential for transforming discourse and relationships.

It all started one evening, when the employers' representatives presented their demand that doctors, like other public-sector employees, should be required to punch a clock. When asked to explain why, the employers' representatives sharply criticized doctors' work ethic. They alleged that, according to data collected in state hospitals, full-time senior doctors and departmental and unit heads were rarely in the hospital for the whole working day. Instead, they regularly left early in the afternoon to attend to their private practice, leaving patients in the hands of interns. The only way to monitor doctors' presence at work was by introducing a system that required all doctors to clock in and out.

The rhetoric of the presentation was an attack on doctors' professional integrity and commitment. The employers' representatives, especially those from the Division of Budget at the Finance Ministry, said that the only reason doctors had been against the idea of monitoring their presence at the hospitals was that it would interfere with their freedom to work outside during regular working hours. They further contended that the majority of doctors kept their admittedly low-paying jobs at public hospitals only as a means to advance their lucrative private practices.

The IMA representatives were furious. They could hardly wait for their turn to speak. All asked to talk at once. We told the doctors that we appreciated the fact that they had internalized the rules of mediation; they had listened patiently to serious allegations impugning their professional integrity and did not interrupt the employers' presentation. Although it was very late, we asked the parties to stay longer. We felt it would be a major mistake to adjourn without giving the doctors the opportunity to respond on the spot.

The IMA leaders said that had the employers' demand been based only on the principle of uniformity, i.e., a requirement that all public-sector employees should punch a clock, it would have been legitimate and understandable. What they could not tolerate and utterly rejected was the outrageous and baseless attack on their commitment to public health care and their professional integrity. According to the IMA leaders, the allegations were not only insulting; they demonstrated a lack of understanding and appreciation of doctors' work, their personal sacrifice and round-the-clock commitment to their

job and their profession. They further complained that the employers' in-
flammatory presentation signaled a step back to the hard-line negotiation tac-
tics that had preceded the mediation.

Once all the IMA's representatives had an opportunity to talk and vent their
anger, we adjourned the meeting. The level of tension and animosity was at
its peak. With very few exceptions, the participants left the room without saying goodnight.

We began the next morning session by reflecting on last night's events. We
asked the employers' representatives whether they were able to recognize that
the doctors had been profoundly offended, and whether they would like to address the IMA representatives on the matter of their hurt feelings.

The Director of the Wage and Labor Agreements Division asked to speak.
He said that although he had not taken part in the previous night's session, he
had received a full account of the heated exchange. He then apologized on behalf of the employers, and retracted the derogatory statements about the doctors' professional commitment and integrity.

The IMA representatives were astonished by the gesture. Both parties were
beginning to experience the effect of the mediation process. The sincere nature of the apology and its acceptance by IMA representatives transformed
the discourse and the relationship from combative to cooperative.

We were ready to continue with the parties' presentations. The time clock
was not mentioned again . . .

The presentations took most of the first week. At the end, to test our understanding of what had been said, we summarized the dispute, as we understood it. We found some comfort in the fact that the four unresolved issues
from the 1994 agreement held the promise of quick resolution, and that we
could identify a major issue—pensions—which had the potential of creating
a breakthrough in the negotiations. There was one key outcome that the Government, or more precisely the Director of the Wage and Labor Agreements
Division, wanted to achieve in the mediation. This was the gradual transfer of
state-employed doctors to a contributory pension fund. For years the Government had been trying to reach agreement on this issue with other public-
sector unions without success. To succeed with the IMA would establish an
important precedent.

What was worrying was the list of what we perceived to be the barriers to
resolution:

(a) At the heart of the dispute were two unresolved public policy questions.
The first was the tension between public and private health care. The second
concerned the effort of the Government to channel the provision of health
care services to HMO clinics. These policy issues were not (and could not be)

the subject of this contract negotiation, yet they were likely to have significant impact on the mediation.

(b) Related to these policy questions, and similarly unresolved, was the issue of doctors' private practice outside and inside hospitals.

(c) The level of trust among the parties was low.

(d) The heterogeneity and the diversity of interests within each side would present substantial difficulties and challenges.

(e) Not only were we mediating a multi-employer collective agreement, but even among the representatives of the state there were noticeably diverging interests and agendas. The Ministry of Health's representatives had the narrowest perspective. Their primary concern was the suffering of the public, especially the low-income population, which could not afford private medical care. They wanted to see a quick end to the strike and were willing to make concessions. They also believed that improving working conditions might help attract and keep good doctors in the public system.

The Wage and Labor Agreements Division had a broader view. At the negotiation table they presented three sets of interests. First, they represented the state, which employed over 3,000 doctors. Second, they were concerned with the likely impact of the negotiations on other public and semi-public employers in the health care sector.[7] Third, the Director of the Wage and Labor Agreements Division's had to take into account the potential impact on *all* public-sector employees; whatever happened in these negotiations would not only affect other employee groups in the health care (i.e., nurses, service and maintenance staff and technicians) but would also affect academics, teachers, engineers, and non-academic university employees.

The officials representing the Division of Budget at the Finance Ministry had the broadest perspective. They had to worry about the well-being not only of the hospitals and clinics that were owned and operated by the state, by Clalit and by Hadassah, but also about the two other sick funds not currently at the table, and, in addition, they had to keep in mind national budgetary considerations.

(f) The IMA leaders had significant secondary interests. They faced an upcoming elections. In fact, the original date of the elections had been postponed because of the strike. In addition, the IMA leadership faced strong internal opposition from a group of senior doctors, fueled primarily by young doctors and militant interns in the ranks of the IMA membership.

(g) The IMA had been spoiled during the previous round of negotiations in 1994. Without having to apply too much pressure, it had been able to convince the Finance Minister to agree to a 60% salary increase.[8] The impact of this very generous concession was reflected in a hardened Government position in the current negotiations. The mediation was conducted just one year after general elections which had brought back to power the Labor Party and the same Finance Minister who had made the concession in 1994. Six years on, the Finance Minister was extremely cautious, since he had been highly criticized for the 1994 deal, which many claimed had dismantled the Government's restrictive wage policy and swept the entire public sector into an unnecessary wave of salary increases.[9]

(h) Ultimately, of course, the key issue was pay. Interns earned five dollars per hour, departmental heads with twenty-five years' of seniority earned a mere ten dollars per hour. The IMA went on strike both to overhaul the remuneration scheme and to double salaries across the board.

The real problem, however, was not low wages. We learned that a convoluted compensation scheme was responsible for the low wages. A substantial part of doctors' income came from hours during which they were on duty or on call after they had completed their regular working day. The 1994 collective agreement provided for a multiplier of five for on-duty hours and a multiplier of three and a half for on-call hours. It also assured the allocation of on-duty and on-call shifts among the hospital doctors on a departmental basis. Furthermore, doctors who occupied managerial positions (general managers, departmental heads, heads of units) were entitled to an on-call allowance for each regular working day. These allowances were called "super on-call," since they actually required no work from the doctors in addition to their regular schedule.

This compensation system had developed during previous contract negotiations. It was primarily a defensive measure, designed to prevent other unions from demanding wage parity with the doctors, the assumption being that since only doctors had to be on duty or on call as part of their job, increasing on-duty and on-call allowances would not spill over to other employee groups. Another reason for the proliferation of on-duty and on-call payments was that they were not subject to social benefits, which made them 30% less expensive for employers than regular wages.

For the doctors, these on-duty and on-call payments created a host of problems. First, the payments were not made during vacation, sick leave and study days (when doctors were away attended conferences, workshops and seminars). At such times, they were entitled only to their base salary. Second, according to the Civil Service Pension Law, on-duty and on-call payments are not pensionable. State doctors were entitled to pension allowances that were calculated taking into account their base salary only. Third, all benefits based on a percentage of doctors' salary, such as those relating to provident funds,[10] continuing education funds[11] and severance pay are calculated taking account of the base salary only. Fourth, the doctors contended that, much like other white-collar employees, and in fact as a matter of principle, their work during the regular working day entitled them to a much higher salary, one that reflected their education and status. Hence, extra payments, paid with respect to hours that exceeded the regular working day, should not be taken into account when comparing doctors' salaries with those of other professionals. Fifth, the hourly rate, which appeared on their pay slip, constantly reminded the doctors of the huge gap between, on the one hand, their social status, and, on the other, their economic status. It was a regular and painful reminder of the low return on their investment in education and training.

The reader must keep in mind that the negotiations took place at the height of the high-tech and dot-com boom. At that time, the young interns understandably compared themselves to their classmates who had gone into hi-tech, where salaries were three times higher and the working day was shorter. And looking at senior doctors' paychecks, the future did not look much brighter. Their salaries also suggested a bleak future for the medical profession and for the continued ability of medical schools to attract the best and the brightest. Finally, even when on-duty and on-call payments were included, most doctors still had to moonlight in order to support their families. Doctors repeatedly complained about disappointment with their professional choice.

This predicament explained why the IMA had gone on strike to double hourly rates of pay, to overhaul the compensation package and, as an interim measure, to expand the salary base used for calculating all benefits, including on-duty and on-call payments.

The employers were unable to offer even a compromise figure. To keep inflation down, the Government had committed to a strict wage policy. Negotiated wage increases were limited to the expected rate of inflation for the term of all contracts. For the doctors, this meant a four-year contract and a five percent increase. The Government was especially worried that any wage increases for doctors would likely be followed by a demand for similar increases from other health service employees, especially from the two militant unions—the Association of Nurses and the Association of Hospital Clerical and Maintenance Workers, both affiliated with the Histadrut.

The employers were sympathetic to the doctors' request to expand the base for calculating benefits. The employers agreed that, due to the fact that base salaries for purposes of calculating benefits excluded on-duty and on-call payments, pension allowances for state-employed doctors, as well as payments for sick leave and study leave, were intolerably low.

Nevertheless, since payments for on-duty and on-call constituted two-thirds of doctors' income, to incorporate them into the salary base for the purpose of calculating benefits would mean an enormous increase in total labor costs, especially indirect costs such as pensions and sick leave.

In recent years, the Division had introduced a profound change in public sector negotiations. The traditional concept of a wage increase had been replaced by a new concept: increased cost. The Division calculated the direct and indirect costs, as well as short- and long-term costs, associated with every demand for a wage increase or other change in salary or benefits. Consequently, when the employers said that under the Government's policy they could offer the doctors five percent, it meant that the total costs of all contractually agreed changes (covering both base and benefits) could not exceed five percent.

A rough calculation indicated that the cost of addressing the state-employed doctors' concerns regarding pensions by making on-duty and on-call payments pensionable would far exceed the five percent limit and would not leave room for any wage increase. In other words, the doctors' request to include payments for on-duty and on-call in the calculation of benefits was a major cost item.

Finding a solution that would be acceptable to all and, at the same time, to address the issue of low hourly rates and the convoluted salary and benefits structure, was a seemingly insurmountable task.

NOTES

1. The education allowance is additional compensation that is paid in recognition of and/or to promote advanced education and training.

2. Both sides listed these four issues among their demands.

3. The bipartite or parity committee is probably the most important and frequently used mechanism for settling labor disputes in Israel. Usually these committees are the central pillar of a typical grievance procedure, and can be found in various forms in almost all collective agreements. Although these bipartite committees have achieved their fame in resolving "right disputes," the very nature of the proceeding have made them equally acceptable for resolving "interest disputes". As the name suggests, the bipartite committees consist of equal numbers of representatives (usually only one or two) from labor and management. These representatives are neither neutrals nor partisan arbitrators. Being a dyad decision-making body, all decisions must be unanimous. The procedure operates as an informal small-scale negotiation session between the parties' appointees, who maintain a close contact with the disputants but are somewhat removed from the dispute. There is a large body of case law in which the labor courts have recognized the unique role of these bipartite committees in resolving labor disputes. See *City of Tel Aviv v. Saar* (1971) 3 P.D.A.160.

4. Richard A. Walton & Robert B. McKersie, *A Behavioral Theory of Labor Negotiations—An Analysis of a Social Interaction System* 5, 144–159 (1965).

5. For the participants, this was probably the most demanding task throughout the mediation.

6. The phrase and the concept are adopted from Carol Liebman, "Mediation as Parallel Seminars: Lessons from the Student Takeover of Columbia University's Hamilton Hall" 16 *Neg.J.* 157, 163. (2000).

7. With the exception of private hospitals and clinics, the Wage and Labor Agreements Division closely supervises all contract negotiations affecting doctors' wages and working conditions.

8. In 1994 Israel had an expected annual inflation rate of about 10%. Hence a 60% increase over a four year contract represented a 5% rate of increase over expected inflation.

9. The annual inflation rate in 2000 was close to zero.

10. The employer's contribution to the provident fund is usually 5% of the employee's monthly salary.

11. The employer's contribution to the continuing education fund is usually 7.5% of the employee's monthly salary.

Chapter Six

Post-Seminar Mediation

At the beginning of the second week of mediation we decided to start operating on two parallel tracks: we would continue the learning process for parties and mediators, but at the same time we would also start helping the parties reach agreement on secondary matters, mindful all the while of possible solutions to the major issues.

In the second week, the learning process regarding health care and doctors' working conditions was somewhat different. This time, we reached out to people who were not part of the mediation. This took us away from the negotiation table.

Experts were invited to our sessions, adding new dimensions to the explanations that we had previously heard. For example, the Assistant Head of the Capital Market Division at the Finance Ministry provided us with a detailed analysis of the costs associated with expanding the salary base for computing pensions. Another example was a meeting between one of our assistants and a prominent professor who specialized in labor economics and who had just finished a longitudinal study of doctors' salaries. Most but not all of the meetings were initiated by the parties to the mediation, or were at least approved by them. The people who met with us volunteered their time.

In addition, we met with other people, primarily from the medical community, who had asked to meet with us. We believed that turning them down would be wrong. They cared about the dispute; what they had to say might shed new light or provide new perspectives.

Entering the second week, we doubted whether we had captured the whole picture. There were a host of unanswered questions. In addition, we had been presented with conflicting answers regarding the issues and the interests behind them. These new educational sessions and informal meetings helped us form a better understanding of the context underlying the dispute.

The need for informal meetings with outside people in order to gather additional information proved how wise our decision to enlarge the mediation team had been.

At the same time that we continued our informal meetings, we pursued a second route which was designed to let the parties explore possible solutions to the major issues and to find out whether they could make progress or reach agreement on minor points. For this activity we relied primarily on private caucuses with each group and joint meetings with small groups of IMA and employer representatives. Since the mediation was conducted in hotels with multiple conference rooms, we were able to make maximum use of our four-member mediation team and work simultaneously on several fronts.

In terms of process, the sessions went well. There was a high level of trust between the two parties, as well as between them and the mediation team. Even the idea of small groups working with a single mediator on a particular issue was well received. Nonetheless, we did not sense progress. *Something was holding the parties back.*

At first, we attributed the lack of progress to mistrust of the figures in the database provided by the Wage and Labor Agreements Division. Everyone had agreed on the need for transparency, and there was a procedure in place for exchanging data, yet we were getting bitter complaints about the data that was supplied. The data related only to state-employed doctors, who counted for one-third of the doctors on strike. The fact that the majority of the doctors (most notably, those employed by Clalit) had significantly different working conditions did not allow for extrapolation from the data available. Another complaint, one that was much more difficult to deal with, was the IMA's unverifiable criticism that the database was unreliable. The third complaint was that the methodology employed by the Division to analyze the economic implications associated with proposed changes in salaries and benefits was inherently flawed.

Our own feeling was that the staff of the Wage and Labor Agreements Division had been highly professional and deserved credit for developing a sophisticated methodology of analyzing costs. However, assessing the total long-term cost of a collective agreement, especially one that applied to 13,000 doctors who, for economic purposes, were divided into numerous groups, raised a host of questions about data collection and methods of aggregation. There were also questions about the assumptions and the methodology of the analysis of costs. The controversy regarding the data and cost analysis was a sticking point for a long time. The problem was not alleviated when the database for Clalit's doctors finally arrived. The Government's Data

Processing Unit needed two additional weeks to harmonize the two sets of data before analysis could begin.

This problem persisted throughout much of the mediation, causing unnecessary tension between the parties, and, unfortunately, also between two members of the mediation team and the staff of the Wage and Labor Agreements Division. To ameliorate the situation we took two steps. A direct line of communication was established between my co-mediator and the Wage and Labor Agreements Division. Later on we also formed a tripartite task force to work on these problems, comprised of one representative from the Wage and Labor Agreements Division, the IMA's accountant and one of our assistant mediators. This task force was expanded in the latter stages of the mediation. Throughout the process it was referred to as the "Economic Table."

Beyond the tensions associated with the database and data analysis, we were convinced that there was something more serious that was holding the parties back. We did not know how to find out what it was. Nevertheless, we were convinced that something was standing in the way of an agreement. It had to be dealt with in order to get the mediation rolling.

Late into the second week, we started to play with two completely new ideas. These ideas would turn out eventually not only to be the central pillars of the final settlement, but they would also emerge as the means for transforming labor and employment relations in public medicine.

Chapter Seven

The Ideas that Matter

In the midst of struggling through the second week, it dawned on us that merely talking about the unresolved issues would not lead to a resolution. This conclusion was premised on several observations, and led us to put forward to the parties two new ideas for their consideration. These ideas had been on our mind from the first days of the mediation. We had had occasion to mention them to the leaders of the parties in private conversations, but during the second week we began to bring them gradually to center stage. The essence of these ideas follows.

THE PUBLIC COMMISSION

The more we learned about the public health care system and how doctors were trained, placed, promoted, compensated, motivated and disciplined, the more we felt that the system was ailing badly and in need of repair. The problem was far broader than the convoluted compensation structure, and involved, among other things, issues of budgeting, staffing, organizational structure, pricing policies and the absence of a clear distinction between public health care and private practice and in public hospitals and outside them.

As the mediation began to produce new ideas and creative solutions, it became evident that it would be impossible to implement them. At times, one or both parties appeared willing to experiment with something new, but the willingness would quickly fade away. We sensed that the parties did not believe there was enough institutional flexibility in the public health care system to embrace change. To change the status quo was a daunting task.

Public health care and medical practice appeared to be a complex inter-
connected web, a patchwork of policies, rules, procedures, practices and
local arrangements that had developed over the years. Due to the way in
which elements in the system interlocked, as well as the wide range of working conditions and remuneration packages of doctors, any meaningful change
in one place in the system would likely cause problems up and down the line.
Three examples will illustrate the point.

The first involved an IMA suggestion to introduce the concept of a "full-
timer,"[1] a doctor who would commit his or her full working week exclusively
to the hospital or clinic where he or she was employed. In return, the full-
timer's salary would be substantially higher, compensating for any forgone
supplementary income which might otherwise be earned from outside work.
The term "full-timer" was actually a misnomer, since many doctors who already occupied full-time positions used to moonlight or run private practices.
Nevertheless, the concept appeared promising and "value-creating".[2] It was
aimed at improving the quality of medical care and doctor-patient relations,
as well as reducing the need for doctors to moonlight and engage in private
practice.

Although the idea was refreshing and served many interests, it did not go
far.[3] It was soon removed from the table as unfeasible. We tried hard to understand why the parties thought it would not work. The principal explanation was that introducing the concept of a "full-timer" meant too much
change, and that it would complicate the existing system. We also had the
sense that the idea received the cold shoulder because many hospitals' doctors were moonlighting in Clalit clinics. If our hypothesis was correct, the
idea of the "full-timer" was partly a victim of the aforementioned unresolved
public policy issue of allocating public health care between the hospitals, on
one hand, and the local clinics, on the other hand.

The second example was the attempt to increase hourly wages in return
for reducing the multipliers used to calculate on-duty and on-call payments. Low hourly wages were the impetus for the strike. The employers
insisted that whatever the outcome of the negotiations, increased compensation would be made in lump sum payments rather than increases in
hourly wages. The underlying reason was that even small increases in
hourly wages would mean larger increases in total health care costs due to
the multipliers. In our search for a mutually acceptable solution, we asked
the Wage and Labor Agreements Division to run several simulations of the
impact of alternative proposals for simultaneous changes in hourly rates
and in the multipliers.

The results demonstrated that the complexity of the system and the diversity of the doctor population made even a seemingly simple change in hourly

wage rates prohibitive. It would, for instance, substantially reduce the income of doctors who worked in hospitals outside the big metropolitan areas. On-duty and on-call work at these hospitals was less demanding, due to the relatively smaller intake of patients. Consequently, doctors in non-metropolitan areas worked, on average, many more on-duty and on-call shifts than doctors in metropolitan hospitals. Since these hospitals tended to be always understaffed, any reduction in doctors' total income would have a negative effect on the ability of hospitals outside the big metropolitan areas to attract and keep doctors. The result of the simulations revealed that, given the existing high multipliers and the requirement to keep total income intact, it was impossible to find a single formula that would balance an increase in hourly rate with a decrease in the multipliers. In other words, any formula that would benefit doctors in metropolitan hospitals would reduce the income of doctors in hospitals outside metropolitan areas. We suggested compensating the latter for the lost income with, say, a sabbatical. The parties said that this would not be feasible.

The third example concerned the issues that had been left open in the 1994 agreement. To address these issues we formed small groups, consisting of representatives of the IMA and the employers, each working with one mediator. Since both sides had vested interests in introducing these long over due changes, the parties easily reached consensus as to how changes would be implemented. Nevertheless, none of these interesting integrative solutions found their way into the agreement due to budget constraints.

The reactions to the "full-timer" proposal, the inability to change wage rates and multipliers, and the failure to resolve issues relating to the 1994 agreement were indicative of a single strategic problem: the public health care system and its relationship with the medical profession badly needed a systemic overhaul.

This was far too big a project for our mediation. In addition, the pressure to end the strike was growing. Besides, the Finance Ministry refused to recognize the IMA as a legitimate partner for negotiating either strategic and systemic changes in the public health care system or the allocation of public resources to it. For its part, the IMA, which had called the strike to improve wages and social benefits, refused to discuss the most sensitive issues, such as doctors' private practices and norms of conduct. Finally, important stakeholders, such as other health care providers, insurance companies and other interested unions, not to mention the consumers of the public health system, were missing from the table.

We began considering the idea of a public commission, which would be appointed by the Government and whose role would be to study the system as a whole and recommend changes.

THE NO-STRIKE ARBITRATION MODEL

Given the huge gap between the parties' expectations in monetary issues, there were insufficient resources for an economic package that would be acceptable to all. From our private conversations with the Government side, including with the Prime Minister himself, we knew roughly how far the employers were willing to go to avoid an even longer and more damaging strike. It was clear that even if we were able to move them a bit, we would still be very far from the minimum of concessions needed to motivate the doctors to end the strike.

We had to create something new, divorced completely from the substantive issues, which would be valued by all. The first two weeks of the mediation revealed that, for different reasons and in different degrees, the participants in the mediation were unhappy with the two years of negotiations that had preceded the strike and the mediation. It was conceivable that they would welcome a complete restructuring of the way they negotiated contracts. The challenge was to design a model process which, on the one hand, would assure better negotiations, yet, on the other, would provide a mutually acceptable resolution in the event of deadlock. Once we had conceptualized the problem along these lines, the seed of an idea was planted: the doctors would submit future disputes relating to contract negotiations to binding arbitration as a quid pro quo for waiving their right to strike. Was this the seed of a settlement or the seed of peace?

NOTES

1. The idea was initially presented to us by the Prime Minister's personal advisor, Prof. Amiram Carmon.

2. David A. Lax & James K. Sebenius, *The Manager as Negotiator: Bargaining for Cooperation and Competitive Gains* 88–106 (1986); Dean G. Pruitt, *Negotiation Behavior* 137–162 (1981).

3. A somewhat different idea referred to as a "personal doctor" suffered a similar fate.

Chapter Eight

The Power of New Ideas

At first we discussed the ideas of a public commission and binding arbitration among ourselves. Although we had only a rough outline in mind, we decided to try these concepts out on the parties' leaders. Subsequently we raised them with the Prime Ministers' Chief of Staff and the Cabinet Secretary. After all, we were aware that if these suggestions were accepted, only arbitration would become part of an agreement; the public commission would not. The latter had to be an important part of the deal as a whole but could not be part of the contract itself. The authority to appoint a public commission derived from the Government's sovereign power, not from any contractual obligation.

As we expected, these ideas affected all aspects of the negotiations. They introduced a new momentum and opened possibilities of resolution. While negotiations over substantive issues continued, the parties and their advisors also carefully considered the two ideas, which addressed long-term, broad, relational and strategic issues, rather than short-term, narrow, substantive and tactical concerns.

Naturally, the novel idea of arbitration as a strike substitute drew the most attention. The employers concentrated mainly on the arbitration proposal, while the IMA focused on the strike ban. It was primarily the Government that vehemently opposed as a matter of principle the idea of relinquishing its decision-making power to a non-governmental arbitration body. From the start, we were cognizant of the fact that to convince the state to submit to arbitration which carried budgetary implications was a tall order. We also assumed that it would require the personal intervention of the Prime Minister and the Attorney General.

Having said that, there was still a good chance that the state would not have to face the dilemma whether or not to relinquish its decision-making powers to an arbitration process. This was because everyone, the Prime Minister's Chief of Staff and the Cabinet Secretary included, believed that it was highly unlikely that the doctors would relinquish their right to strike. We also believed that convincing the doctors to abandon this traditional source of power and put their fate in the hands of an unknown arbitration procedure was going to be an uphill challenge. And indeed it was.

Chapter Nine

The Crisis: We Were Leaving

The third week of the mediation began with a love-fest. The parties had fallen in love with the process. No one except us seemed to remember that it had been agreed that the mediation would last no more than two-to-three weeks. But we did . . .

Mediation sessions were conducted daily. It appeared that negotiations were finally starting to produce new options, interesting concessions, and tentative agreements. Nevertheless, the gap on the monetary issues was still very wide.

The IMA agreed in principle that a change in hourly wage rates might have to wait. The employers were willing to increase the cost of the agreement to 13.25 percent, provided the new contract ran for four and a half years, i.e. until the end of 2002 (calculated from the date of termination of the previous agreement). The IMA demanded a much higher figure for a shorter contractual term—no more than three years. There was tentative agreement that salary increases would be in the form of lump-sum monthly payments, and that these increases would not be the same across the board. The most underpaid (the interns) would receive the largest increase; departmental heads would receive the smallest. This inverse distribution of wage increase could be attributed to the transformation, which the IMA delegation was undergoing during the mediation. It had to face an unfair salary ladder, under which young doctors felt exploited in terms of both workload and income distribution.

The parties were working hard to find creative and mutually acceptable solutions to the problems of reduced income during vacation, sick leave and study time.

The Prime Minister called us for an informal meeting at his official Jerusalem residence. He wanted an update and a prognosis. He also wanted

31

to give us his point of view. His personal advisor, Professor Carmon, and the Cabinet Secretary were part of the meeting. At the request of the Prime Minister's staff, we prepared a document outlining alternative courses for resolving the strike. They included our ideas about a public commission and arbitration.

Since we had an initial response to these ideas from the IMA, we expressed optimism regarding the prospect of convincing the IMA to give up the right to strike. The Prime Minister admonished us that a settlement that substantially deviated from the national wage policy would undermine the Government's macro-economic goals of continued growth and low inflation.

We also arranged a meeting between the IMA leaders and the Prime Minister's Chief of Staff. It was important for the IMA leaders to hear his prognosis as well. In the course of the meeting, the Prime Minister's Chief of Staff heard first-hand that the IMA was interested in the two ideas we had proposed. Prior to that point he had doubted the IMA would ever consider giving up the right to strike.

As the third week came to a close, Miki approached me with a surprising observation. He was convinced that the parties felt too comfortable with the mediation process. Consequently, they were dragging their feet and wearing us down with repeated presentations, arguments and computations. With our assistance, they had made progress on some of the issues. In his opinion, however, they were still far from reaching agreement, while we as mediators had reached the point of diminishing returns. He suggested that we convene the parties, provide them with a mediators' proposal, and leave the scene.

I tended to agree, but felt uneasy with Miki's suggested course of action. It ran against my instincts. After all, as a mediator I was used to staying with the process, empowering and inspiring the disputants, nurturing the prospect of settlement, infusing the process with endless optimism and faith in the parties' ability to reach agreement on their own, rather than imposing my solution. In terms of Riskin's grid[1] I consider myself a facilitative-broad mediator. I generally try to avoid as much as possible giving proposals to the parties. But here we were considering not only offering the parties a mediators' proposal, but also leaving if they did not accept it.

Nevertheless, I decided to go along. It felt right. We sat down to plan the meeting and to formulate our proposal.

The mediators` proposal consisted of two parts. First, there were substantive terms of settlement. Second, there was the Public Commission comprised of experts appointed by the Prime Minister and the Minister of Health, combined with arbitration as a strike substitute. Our proposals were in outline only; the details were left for the parties.

The substantive terms that we proposed were as follows: (1) a monetary package of 13 percent in total costs; (2) a salary increase of NIS 3,000 (approximately $750) per month for interns and a sliding scale of salary increases up to NIS 1,000 (approximately $250) per month for departmental heads; (3) salary increases would be part of the salary base for the calculations of benefits and would not be used for computing on-duty and on-call payments; (4) 60 percent of total income would be pensionable; (5) only sick leave allowance would be based on total regular income; (6) paid vacation and days off for continuing education would be based on the newly defined pensionable income; (7) payment of a further education allowance; (8) establishing a common database that would be accepted by all parties; (9) assembling an abridged version of all applicable collective agreements.

We presented our proposal orally. We preferred not to produce a written document outlining our proposal, as it was important to assure the parties and the public that we were in mediation, not in arbitration. In order to test their reaction, we decided to announce our decision to end the mediation and to present our proposal to separate meetings of the full delegations. Subsequently we convened a joint session with both delegations.

We opened each session by complementing the participants' commitment to the mediation and their achievements thus far. We reminded them that they had allotted two to three weeks to the mediation. That time was now at an end. We felt that our ability to assist was at an end too. Thus, we decided to end our involvement as mediators. We preferred to do so at the height of our contribution, rather than to continue in a process with diminishing returns. We added that since the mediation had been at the Prime Minister's initiative, we would notify him personally that the mediation had run its course.

Nevertheless, we told the parties that we wished to share with them our proposal for a settlement. We cautioned them to listen to our proposal neither as an advisory arbitration award nor as a conciliation report, but as a possible framework for solution. We underscored that the proposal was not intended to reflect what we believed to be the right solution. Instead, our proposal was intended to reflect what we believed the parties could live with. We explained the proposed terms of settlement and described the philosophy underlying the Public Commission and the arbitration.

We said that we were not surprised that they had been unable to reach a settlement. The dispute was complicated, and the solution would also be complicated; the problems were deeply rooted. It would be impossible to solve them in a single stroke.

What we proposed was a multi-stage dynamic solution. The first stage was intended to be an immediate, although partial, solution to the most pressing problems. The second stage was long-term, and was aimed at dealing with strategic issues. The former was results-oriented and the latter process-focused.

We indicated that the Public Commission and the arbitration were entirely new in the public health care system. We added that, thus far, the parties had not given these ideas the attention we thought they deserved. We thought these ideas were the mediation's most important contribution to an improved employment and labor relations environment.

We closed the session by thanking everyone for trusting us, for their openness, and for their cooperation. When the members in each team realized that we were leaving, they were stunned.

During the joint session the participants went out of their way to praise the mediation. Although we had made only little progress, they complemented the process. They enjoyed the experience—new to them, in what was, after all, a two-year-long negotiation—of being able to converse in a non-confrontational way. They felt that, free from the pressure from the media, they had all made huge progress in terms of their ability to listen to the other party and their willingness to recognize that the points that the other party was raising might have validity. We were happy to learn that one of the IMA leaders, who had been among the most skeptical at the beginning, now saw the mediation as the key to keeping the parties in the process and to changing their discourse. In his view, the parties were still far apart but moving in the right direction. Others impressed us by the extent they had internalized the premise of the mediation process. They said we had been emphasizing throughout the mediation that it was a voluntary process. Anyone could leave. This included the mediators.

Finally, the parties spoke for the first time about the Public Commission and the arbitration. The Director of the Wage and Labor Agreements Division said that he disliked the idea of a public commission. Only the Government was authorized to decide whether to appoint a public commission. In principal, the Government's position on arbitration was also negative. Nevertheless, given the fact that all the alternatives were bad, the Director and other officials from the Finance Ministry wanted to study the idea further before the Prime Minister made a final decision. At that stage, they were not ready to give an educated response.

The IMA said that, in contrast to the Government, they were ready. They had less need to consult with advisors and to study the arbitration model, as its outside legal counsel had written extensively about dispute resolution and arbitration.[2] The problem for the IMA was the realization that the employers (including the Government) had failed to see the no-strike arbitration idea as a possible achievement in the negotiation. As a result, the employers were unwilling to give value in exchange for what the IMA saw as a major sacrifice—waiving its right to strike.

The leaders agreed to a joint resolution: (a) the parties asked that the mediation be suspended rather than terminated; (b) the parties wanted time to study the mediators' proposal; (c) the parties wanted the mediators to be part of the deliberations regarding the mediators' proposal, and to meet with their constituencies and the decision-makers; (d) in the interim, the mediators were asked to share their proposal with the Prime Minister and report to him the decision to suspend the mediation; and (e) the parties wanted the mediators to consider resuming the mediation after the parties had concluded their deliberations. In retrospect, our decision to leave probably had a positive effect on the succeeding stages of the mediation. It had shock value and it introduced a sense of urgency.

NOTES

1. Leonard Riskin, "Mediator Orientation, Strategies and Techniques", 12 *Alternative to the High Cost of Litigation.* (1994) 111; Leonard Riskin,"Understanding Mediators' Orientation, Strategies, and Techniques: A Grid for the Perplexed" 1 *Harv. Neg. L. Rev.* 7 (1996).

2. See for example: Frances Raday, *Adjudication of Interest Disputes* (1983).

Chapter Ten

Back to Study

During the next seven days, no mediation sessions were held. Nevertheless, this was an intense time for the mediators. Our focus could be summed up in one concept: no-strike arbitration.

The Director of the Wage and Labor Agreements Division wasted no time engaging us. The next day we were invited to the Finance Ministry to address a large group of officials. Representatives from the Finance Ministry's Division of Budget and the Division were present. The Ministry of Justice, and in particular the Ministry's Department of Labor Disputes, also sent representatives.

We presented the outline of the proposed arbitration procedure and answered questions. Many of the comments concerned studies about arbitration, especially interest arbitration abroad.[1] The level of suspicion and hostility towards the idea was high. No one seemed to care about the strike ban, which was designed to appeal to the Government. All they wanted to talk about and to dispose of was the arbitration element of our proposal.

This was understandable. The Finance Ministry's officials and their lawyers had three main concerns: (1) an arbitration board might not be bound by national economic and wage policies; (2) an arbitration award could have far-reaching labor relations and budgetary ramifications which the Government would have to accept; and (3) arbitration meant delegating governmental authority to non-public officials.

For the officials the arbitration concept was new. Israel had virtually no experience with interest arbitration, especially not with the tripartite arbitration board we had in mind. In fact, Israel had very little experience with labor arbitration at all. There had been very few awards by private arbitrators in the public sector. One or two were still remembered as particularly costly. There was also no precedent for a union giving up its right to strike.

There was however one experiment which might prove helpful, the Institute of Voluntary Arbitration in the Public Service ("IVAPS"). Established in 1977 by the Histadrut and the state, the IVAPS was entrusted with broad jurisdictional authority. It was headed by a highly respected former Supreme Court Justice, and, after a ceremonious inauguration, it began its activity to general high expectations. Sadly, however, the IVAPS had become a white elephant.[2] It heard few cases, and those were of marginal importance. Notwithstanding the existence of the IVAPS, the vast majority of labor disputes in the public sector were resolved through protracted negotiation following strikes.

The more we talked, the more we felt that we had hit rock bottom. As a last resort, I added that if the Government did not seize the opportunity to introduce non-confrontational methods of dispute resolution and continued to yield only to extortion and force, it would be blamed for encouraging the rule of force and violence.

At the end of the three-hour meeting we noted the following: (1) the Government was studying the arbitration component in depth; (2) the two ministries had formed a joint team for that purpose; and (3) only one attorney from the Division had a positive reaction to our no-strike arbitration proposal. She felt the innovative idea deserved serious consideration. The others were clearly against it.

Having an optimistic outlook (which goes with the trade), we were happy to discover even a single ray of light. We also sensed throughout the meeting that the lawyer representing the Wage and Labor Agreements Division was expressing not only her view but also the opinion of the Director of the Division.

This meeting marked the beginning of a long series of seminars that we conducted with people who were not members of the negotiation teams but who became instrumental in the mediation process. Among them were ministers, members of governing bodies, professionals and their constituencies. We were open to meeting anyone who wanted to see us. We held many such meetings during these ten days and throughout the mediation.

Several days were spent with the doctors. We had separate meetings with the IMA leadership, its advisors, the IMA negotiation team, and with doctors who held no particular position in the IMA.

We were happy to discover that the parties' pledge of confidentiality and the media blackout were holding. With the exception of the negotiation team, no one seemed to fully understand the details of our proposal. The parties wanted time to study our proposal. We were supposed to do the teaching. Instead we ourselves were being educated.

The IMA was determined to use this period of time to influence the design of the Public Commission and the no-strike arbitration model. We happily concluded that the leadership and the negotiation team had made the strategic decision to accept the idea. The IMA was starting to see the proposed settlement as a three-step process. The first step was settlement of the immediate conflict, while the third step was the arbitration. But it was the second step they proposed, an interesting idea which they referred to as "the anchor," which was problematic. We were disappointed to hear the idea, and even more so to learn that the IMA insisted on linkage. It would accept the arbitration model only with the anchor. For the IMA it was both or none.

The idea underlying the anchor was that there should be a short-term agreement under which all the money that had been allocated under the mediators' proposal to salary increases would be earmarked only for interns, rather than across the board. There would be no change in the base salary of other doctors. Given the fact that interns' salaries were low and that they could hardly have outside income, the idea seemed appealing.

In fact, however, allocating all the funds to interns was not as generous as it appeared. The idea was to enter into a relatively short-term agreement with an irrational salary scale without differentials between interns and seniors. The assumption was that the Public Commission or the arbitration board would be likely to open up salary differentials. Given the increase in interns' salaries, however, everyone would start from a much higher base.

We exerted considerable efforts to convince the IMA that the anchor was not only unacceptable, but it was also a dangerous tactic. We told the IMA that the ruse was transparent, and that the Director would see through it immediately and might perceive it as a return to the old style of adversarial, bad-faith negotiations (which indeed it was). In addition, politically, it was too risky. The IMA membership and leadership consisted primarily of senior doctors who, under the principle of the anchor, would receive no wage increase. The IMA leaders would have sufficient difficulty explaining to the most successful doctors in the country, who had been on strike for months, that their strike yielded just over $250 a month, let alone if they got no increase at all.

There was another encouraging development during the five days of talks with the doctors. We learned for the first time that the IMA was willing to consider transferring new state-employed doctors to a contributory pension fund, provided pensionable income increased to 70%. We already knew that this issue commanded the highest priority of the Director. The prospect of a successful conclusion seemed brighter.

The rest of our time was spent with the Government. The Prime Minister, other ministers and their staff wanted to study our proposal. While we were teaching, we continued to learn.

Our first meeting was with the Finance Minister and his staff. The discussion focused solely on the arbitration component of the no-strike arbitration proposal. The Ministry decided to fight the idea of submitting budget and wage policy issues to a unaccountable arbitration board whose decisions would bind the Government. He added that both the Attorney General and the Department of Labor Disputes at the Ministry of Justice shared his view.

The next day we were invited for the first time to meet the Minister of Health. Prior to the meeting, the Minister's assistant asked us to prepare an executive summary of our proposal. We explained to him the reasons for our reluctance to commit our proposal to writing. First, our fear that such a document might find its way into the hands of the media, thus violating the principle of confidentiality. Second, a written proposal could be perceived, even mistakenly, as an advisory arbitration award. Third, as long as the proposal remained unwritten it was flexible. When the Minister of Health's assistant insisted, we wrote an executive summary of our proposal for the eyes of the Minister only. It was agreed that we would bring the document with us. The Minister of Health read it carefully and asked questions. He was disturbed by the strike, by the indifference of other Cabinet members, and by the fact that he had all the responsibility and no authority to settle the strike. The Minister promised to try to convince the Cabinet to direct the Director to accept our proposal as a way of bringing the strike to an end.

One may appreciate our frustration when we learned on our way home that at one point in the meeting, when the Minister of Health excused himself from the room, he in fact left the meeting in order to read our document to the TV reporters waiting outside.

The next, and by far the most important, meeting took place the next day in the Prime Minister's office. The Cabinet Secretary reached both of us at our homes early that morning; the Prime Minister wanted to see us at noon. The Cabinet Secretary added that our meeting with the Prime Minister must be kept confidential. We could not disclose it to any one.

While we were driving to Jerusalem, we were surprised when the radio reported our upcoming meeting with the Prime Minister. One explanation for the leak may be that in the six hours that had elapsed, the nature of the meeting had changed from an intimate, informal meeting with the Prime Minister to a larger forum.

Instead of being directed to the Prime Minister's private office, we were ushered into a spacious conference room, where a large meeting was in progress. Present around the table were the Prime Minister, his Chief of Staff, the Cabinet Secretary, the Finance Minister, the Finance Ministry's General Manager, the Head of the Budget Division, the Director of the Wage and Labor Agreements Division, the Minister of Health and the Ministry of Health's General Manager. Also present were various deputies, assistants, and spokespersons.

In all, twenty people faced us. On our way to the meeting we were dismayed to learn that prior to it the Minister of Health, who had previously read our proposal in an interview given to a television reporter, had now gone one step further. His spokesman issued a written press release which contained the executive summary that we had prepared for his eyes only. All our efforts to keep our proposal from ever appearing in writing had been in vain.

When we entered, the Cabinet Secretary handed us a note, which contained the following information: (a) there had been a heated discussion as to whether to adopt the idea of arbitration; (b) those who had spoken vehemently against the idea were winning the debate; (c) only we could sway the room in the other direction.

The Prime Minister asked us to present our case. We said that Israel was facing a historic opportunity. For decades Israeli society had been searching for an acceptable process to end strikes in essential services. The existing means—injunctions and back-to-work emergency regulations—had proven to be legally problematic and inadequate in practice. Over the years, close to thirty bills had been introduced advocating compulsory arbitration as a quid pro quo for the right to strike in essential services.[3] All these bills had failed because of the opposition of the Labor Party and the Histadrut. They had no quarrel with arbitration; their objection was to compelling workers by legislation to give up the right to strike.

As a result of the mediation, we had witnessed an unprecedented event—a union of employees in a essential service was considering giving up the right to strike. The Government had to seize this opportunity to give this experiment and chance to succeed, and to test the proposed voluntary no-strike arbitration model.

Addressing the Finance Ministry's fear of arbitration, I spoke as an expert witnesses. I said that the Government was not facing an unknown and untried path. It could benefit from the extensive experience that had accumulated over many years in other countries, including the United States and Canada, where various models of arbitration had been tried out successfully.

Our idea was certainly not risk-free. I felt, however, that given the alternatives, it was worth taking the risk, and, making use of the accumulated knowledge, designing a state-of-the-art arbitration model which would address the Government's concerns.

I concluded by saying that people in Israel live in a violent region. Life in Israel is tense, full of conflicts and violence. A strike, especially by doctors, is an act of violence. But for the Government not to take serious efforts to end the strike was also a form of violence, albeit a passive one, by permitting interference in the medical wellbeing of its citizens. The Government not only faced an opportunity to change the ailing system of public-sector labor relations, it had a historical opportunity to take leadership in establishing a model of non-violent consensual conflict resolution, premised on reason instead of brute force. Adopting the voluntary no-strike arbitration model would be seen not only as the Government's pledge to care for the health of its citizens, but also as a commitment to non-violence and a better quality of life.

Miki, when he spoke, was extremely effective. After all, the main concern around the table was the price that the Government was asked to pay for a strike ban, namely submitting to arbitration. In practice, it meant a loss of exclusive decision-making power by the state and by the employers in general. Miki was himself one of Israel's major employers and an economist. He himself had worked for several years at the Finance Ministry. He understood what it meant to give up decision-making power. Consequently, his support for the no-strike arbitration was a major achievement, and added credibility to our proposal.

Miki pointed out the successful arbitration system for contract negotiation disputes in the Swiss army, with which he was familiar. Finally, referring to the four issues that had been unresolved since the 1994 contract involving badly needed organizational changes, Miki stressed that, in addition to achieving peace in industrial relations, an arbitration award might bring about gains for the employers, gains which they had been unable to achieve through regular negotiations.

A short discussion followed our presentation. We were encouraged by the questions, which focused on design issues: the composition of the arbitration board, the selection process and arbitrability in general. From the remarks it was clear that it had probably been a mistake to advocate no-strike arbitration without providing further details on the subject. We now explained that we envisioned a tripartite board, one of whose members would be the Director, Furthermore, we believed that the decision-making process of the arbitration board should follow rules and criteria that would be established in advance.

Leaving the room, we were unable to predict the meeting's conclusion. We did not know whether the Finance Ministry had second thoughts. The truth was that it did not matter. Earlier, the Director had told us that the Public Commission option did not belong on the negotiation table, only no-strike arbitration did. The former would be decided by the Prime Minister alone. It was now clear that the issue of no-strike arbitration had also been taken off the table and placed in the hands of the Prime Minister.

Later that day, the Prime Minister's Chief of Staff called and confirmed this. The press reported that the Prime Minister would decide whether to accept no-strike arbitration within thirty-six hours.

The Prime Minister's Chief of Staff summoned us to his office. He admonished us that the Prime Minister was sensitive to the Finance Ministry's fears that an adverse arbitration award or series of awards could affect the

Government's efforts to promote growth and to adhere to the principle of a no-deficit budget. He asked whether we could come up with what he called an "ejection seat" proposal. He mentioned several possibilities. Among them, having the Prime Minister appoint a fourth member of the arbitration board, giving the Prime Minister a veto power over any award, with the understanding that such action would lead to a strike.

We asked whether the Government would be interested in having an agreement on one round of arbitration, as a trial run. We could not think of any other good "ejection seat" proposal which would be consistent with neutrality and finality. After all, an arbitration award could be just as disastrous for the doctors as it could for the Government and the employers. We were in fact encouraged by talk of an "ejection seat." To our ears it sounded as if the Prime Minister was leaning towards accepting the no-strike arbitration model.

Before leaving we asked the Chief of Staff to remind the Prime Minister of two facts we had mentioned during the meeting. The first was that in 1977 the Rabin Government and the Attorney General had signed an arbitration agreement with the Histadrut.[4] At that time, the Histadrut did not agree to a strike ban as a quid pro quo for arbitration. The second was that the Finance Ministry premised its objection to arbitration primarily on the arbitration board's lack of accountability. But to our knowledge, no Minister or any other official had ever been held accountable for granting a salary increase, even in cases where the increase resulted in substantial economic harm to the national economy.

NOTES

1. In many legal systems there is a distinction between interest disputes, sometime referred to as economic or contract negotiation disputes, and grievances, sometimes referred to as right or legal disputes. The former are disputes related to negotiations in which the parties to a collective agreement renegotiate its terms to change the parties' future rights and duties. The latter are disputes over the interpretation and enforcement of existing rights and duties. The distinction is sharper in the United State and Canada than in other legal systems, such as Israel, where unions tend to strike also during the contract. See the Labour Law Casebook Group, *Labour and Employment Law* 6th Ed. 548 (1998); Laura J. Cooper, Dennis R. Nolan & Richard A. Bale, *ADR in the Workplace* 16–17 (2000).

2. Mordehai Mironi, *The Arbitration of Labor Disputes–A Study of the Institute of Voluntary Arbitration in the Public Service* (1988).

3. Mordehai Mironi, "Compulsory Arbitration–Eighty Years of Debate" 1 *Lab. L. Yearbook* 119 (1990).

4. This was the IVAPS agreement, *supra*, note 2.

Chapter Eleven

The Mediation Resumed

The fourth week came to an end and the fifth week began. The parties asked us to resume the mediation, and we agreed. The tone had changed. No-strike arbitration and the Public Commission were on everyone's mind, but had not yet been placed on the negotiating table. Our proposed settlement terms became a single text, providing a focus for the negotiations.

The Director of the Wage and Labor Agreements Division and other employers became more relaxed. The cost of the agreement was not yet known, but was gradually emerging. Another positive development was that finally, after five weeks, the IMA received all the data it had requested.

More importantly, the issue of the doctors' pensions became broader and turned into an integrative issue.[1] The Director saw an opportunity to reach a precedent-setting agreement to move state doctors to a contributory pension fund. Since he could not afford to let this golden opportunity slip, the employers' side became more creative in solving the IMA's goal of increasing the income on which pensions were calculated from 40 percent to 70 percent.

There were, however, some negative developments. The Department of Labor Disputes at the Ministry of Justice delivered an opinion letter to the Prime Minister, with copies to other Ministries, strongly rejecting the idea of arbitration. The opinion reflected the Attorney General's position. This was a setback, and could potentially be a serious problem. The general rule was that any undertaking by the Government to submit to arbitration had to be approved by the Attorney General. In addition, the IMA leadership was having severe difficulties in convincing the local leadership to support the concept that some of the improvements they wanted to see would come in the future via the Public Commission and the arbitration process. The local leaders wanted to show their members immediate results.

Under pressure from both the local leadership and grass-root members, the IMA stated that it would be impossible to settle at 13 percent. It needed at least two percent more.

We convinced the IMA to concede one of the four issues from the 1994 agreement in return for an additional two percent. But the Director of the Wage and Labor Agreements Division refused to accept the trade-off. He reminded us how the 13 percent figure had been arrived at. According to him, the employers had agreed to accept 13 percent on the assumption that the IMA would agree to a long-term contract of five and a half years (until the end of 2003). But the IMA insisted on a shorter, three-and-a-half year term (until the end of 2001). For such a short term the employers had agreed to no more than a 10 percent increase. According to the Director of the Wage and Labor Agreements Division, 13 percent for a three-and-a-half year contract represented a major concession. 13 percent had become the golden number in the negotiations only because the mediators had proposed it. Consequently, 13 percent would remain the ceiling as far as the employers were concerned. We were convinced that this position was strongly held.

The IMA had no new proposals to make. A short-term contract was a high priority. Under these circumstances, the only way for the IMA to improve on the percentage being offered would be by leaving the mediation and escalating the strike. We felt that, as a whole, the IMA had achieved a satisfactory deal, one that had great potential for future gains. We searched for ways to help the IMA leadership to accept the offer.

There were two things we envisioned. The first was to help the IMA face the reality that the 13 percent figure was carved in stone. Trying to extract more was unrealistic. The second was to accept the IMA leaders' invitation to address the members of the IMA governing board and local leaders in order to enlist their support for the proposed settlement.

NOTE

1. As defined by Richard A. Walton & Robert B. McKersie, *A Behavioral Theory of Labor Negotiations—An Analysis of Social Interaction System 5*, 144–159 (1965).

Chapter Twelve

Helping the IMA Accept the Proposed Settlement

It was evident from the beginning that the IMA followed a strategy of placing its trust in the Prime Minister. The Finance Minister and the Director of the Wage and Labor Agreements Division were hardly likely to be the IMA's allies. They had a strict wage policy to adhere to, and they had bad memories of the negative impact of the concessions that had been made to the IMA in the previous round of negotiations (in 1994) on public-sector wages and on the economy in general. The IMA's strategy, therefore, focused on the Prime Minister. Not only would he be sensitive to the suffering of the citizens of the country, he would also have the power to force the Finance Minister and the Director of the Wage and Labor Agreements Division to deviate from their strict wage policy and agree to the IMA's demands.

In view of its strategy of pinning its hopes on the Prime Minister, the IMA leadership had to be absolutely sure that what was being offered was the maximum that the Prime Minister would agree to give. Therefore, we arranged an informal meeting between the Prime Minister, the IMA Chairman and Miki. The Prime Minister convinced the IMA Chairman that nothing more would be offered. As a final gesture, the Prime Minister agreed to an additional 0.2 percent, raising the total to 13.2 percent. Shortly afterwards, the Prime Minister left for an international summit at Camp David with President Clinton and Arafat.

The IMA's dilemma was clear. It could either accept the 13.2 percent or leave the mediation—walk away from what had been achieved and hope that the strike would produce better results. The leadership of the IMA was leaning towards accepting the proposed deal, but it could not proceed unless the proposal was approved by the IMA governing body and had the support of its members.[1] Due to the strike, the internal elections in the IMA had been postponed, and were to be held two months after the strike ended. The current leadership was aware of the strong militant opposition that it faced from interns on one hand and departmental heads on the other.

The IMA convened its 38-member governing body, a large group of officials, local leaders, and strike activists. I was asked to address this meeting to explain the proposed deal, which was comprised of the following: (a) the monetary package, (b) the Public Commission, and (c) the no-strike arbitration model. Miki was away on a business trip. It was a critical moment in the negotiations and a delicate task for me as a mediator.

From the beginning of the mediation process, I had felt that the time might come when I would have to speak directly with the doctors or their local leaders. When that time finally came, I realized that if it backfired, my authority to continue as a mediator would be considerably impaired. Nevertheless, I had to take this risk. I accepted their invitation. It was clear that the ability of the IMA leadership and the negotiation team to get the support of their constituency and to proceed to the final stage depended on this meeting.

I opened with an explanation about mediation and how I saw my role at the meeting. I emphasized that the mediator's role in negotiations was primarily process-oriented, not result-oriented; the parties, not the mediators, were responsible for the outcome and for deciding whether to agree to the proposed settlement.

I saw my role in the meeting as neither to sell the proposed deal nor to give my evaluation or professional advice. These tasks were for the IMA leaders, for experts and for consultants. My role was educational: to share my understanding of the dispute and to explain the proposed settlement terms, especially the ideas underlying the Public Commission and the no-strike arbitration model, and how these two new concepts were connected to the monetary gains of the proposed settlement.

I talked about the economic package. I emphasized that part of the mediator's role was to provide the parties with a reality check, to help them understand the terms of the proposed agreement, how these terms served their needs and interests and what the alternatives to an agreement were.

In contrast to the 1994 agreement, the package now on the table did not offer the doctors, especially the higher ranking doctors who constituted the majority of those present at the meeting, immediate gains in terms of their income. In addition, unlike previous agreements under which all (or at least most) of the money was channeled to across-the-board salary increases that disproportionately benefited those at the upper end of the salary ladder, this proposed package was more egalitarian. It was also interest based, addressing the most urgent needs of the doctors. Consequently, the lion's share of the money would be allocated to salary increases for lower-paid doctors, to improving doctors' pensions and to maintaining doctors' income levels during periods of absence from work such as sickness and study leave.

I admitted that one could easily be disappointed by the 13.2 percent cost figure[2] and the modest salary increase, compared to the doctors' expectations at the beginning of the strike (their initial demands were for an increase of 100 percent in hourly wage rates and treating all income as pensionable). I assured them that I could also empathize with their continued sense that doctors in public health did not enjoy the salaries and working conditions they deserved, based on their responsibility and the sacrifices they made in terms of educational investment and long-term preparation for their profession.

I also shared with them some of my observations. First, that achievements in contract negotiations, especially in the public sector, were never based on justice, equity or merit. Rather, they reflected bargaining power and the reality of what one could achieve under the existing circumstances.

Second, that after hundreds of hours of mediation and long conversations with the Prime Minister and the Finance Minister, I was convinced that the economic package on offer reflected the last available dollar. The Government's position was not based on a belief that doctors did not deserve more, but rather on considerations of overall economic policy. In a period of virtually zero inflation and with a Government committed to promoting privatization and economic growth, there was a deep concern that even a slightly more generous agreement with the doctors might have a devastating macroeconomic impact. It would quickly spill over to other employee groups in the health care industry and the public sector at large. The outcome of negotiations with the IMA had always been perceived as a benchmark, not only for the unions in the health care industry but also for unions in the public sector in general.[3]

Third, in judging the proposed deal, the economic gains should not be separated from the Public Commission and the arbitration, which were the most important achievements of the strike. These new features held real promise for a substantial, albeit not immediate, improvement in doctors' salaries and working conditions.

The rest of my presentation was devoted to reframing the dispute. I said that, in our understanding, the dispute was not only about money. It was about the future status of public health care and the doctors' professional quality of life. Consequently, even if the IMA could improve the proposed economic package by two or three percent by extending or escalating the strike, this would not improve the status of public health care or the conditions under which doctors worked. The death toll and the damage to the health of thousands of citizens would probably damage beyond repair the doctors' image and harm doctor-patient relations.

I added that during the mediation we discovered that the real issue for the doctors was the public health care system. We were addressing only part of a larger problem. Improving doctors' professional quality of life required systemic, long-term changes.

Naturally, such changes could not be dealt with at the negotiating table. However, one of the IMA's major achievements during the mediation was the Government's recognition of the need for change and its commitment to a new course of action. The Government had agreed to establish a Public Commission and charge it with the important task of investigating and recommending changes in public health care, including the status and working conditions of doctors.

The Public Commission's mandate would provide for non-binding recommendations. Nevertheless, experience taught us that well thought-out recommendations were not easily ignored. In particular, these recommendations might set the stage for subsequent negotiations, which might culminate in binding arbitration—the third component of the proposed deal.

The last part of my talk was devoted to reframing the right to strike in the context of the doctors' moral obligations towards their patients. Throughout the mediation we had urged the IMA to reconsider the value of the right to strike. The need for reconsideration had nothing to do with the declining utility of strikes,[4] which was a worldwide phenomenon. It concerned the fact that doctors were not typical employees. They could not be classified with other groups of essential employees. The doctors' intimate contact with their patients' lives and wellbeing put them in an unusual position. At the same time, this relationship constrained their ability to exercise their right to strike. Considering these inhibitions, the doctors faced unique constraints in using strikes or the threat of strikes to exert pressure in contract negotiations.

Exchanging the right to strike for binding arbitration meant that the doctors would no longer rely on their power to withhold services as a means of improving their working conditions. At the same time, the decisions regarding doctors' wages and working conditions would be taken out of the hands of the Finance Ministry and handed to an independent, neutral arbitration board. This was a major and unprecedented achievement for the IMA. The Government and other employers were willing to relinquish their decision-making power for ten years and to entrust individuals who were not public officials with the authority to make binding decisions regarding doctors' salaries and working conditions.

The proposed no-strike arbitration model would replace the power of the strike with the power of reasoning. It would relieve the doctors of the difficult moral dilemma associated with the decision to strike. Being the only group of professional employees to voluntarily give up the right to strike and whose working conditions would be determined by a non-partisan board would enhance the doctors' status. At the same time, the arbitration would insulate any IMA achievements in future rounds of negotiations from becoming a benchmark for demands made by other unions in the public health industry and the public sector at large.

I closed my presentation by saying that, considering the large gap between the IMA's initial demands and what they could get through the negotiation, they had to decide which of two courses to take: (1) to reject the proposed deal and escalate the strike; or (2) to accept the deal and trust that through the Public Commission and the arbitration they would be able to achieve additional gains in the future. I urged them to give serious thought to the proposed settlement, not because it was better or fairer, but because it carried the possibility of future strategic change.

As had been agreed before the meeting with the IMA leadership, I took questions and then left the room before the discussion and ballot. Most of the questions related to the strike ban and what could be expected of the arbitration. Several hours latter I was informed that the proposed deal had been accepted.

We were finally ready to draft and close. Given the complexity of the deal and its innovative components, especially the no-strike arbitration model, we sensed that closure would be an uphill battle. And indeed it was.

NOTES

1. Israel has no ratification process of collective agreements by union members, as it is commonly the case in the United State. See Clyde W. Summers, "Ratification of Agreements" in *Frontiers of Collective Bargaining*, John T. Dunlop & Neil W. Chamberlain Eds. 75 (1967).

2. I explained also that the Director of the Wage and Labor Agreements Division was speaking in terms of cost increase rather than salary increase, and how these new calculations were heavily influenced by actuarial considerations.

3. As the Director of the Wage and Labor Agreements Division had explained to me, the actual number of doctors was relatively small compared to other employee groups, but in the public sector it had always had a disproportionate affect on the Government's ability to carry out its wage policy.

4. James Stern, "Declining Utility of the Strike" 18 *Indus. & Lab. Rel. Rev.* 60 (1964).

Chapter Thirteen

Drafting—The Lawyers' Week

The sixth and last week of the mediation was by far the toughest, both physically and mentally. In theory, it was not supposed to be so hard. After all, agreement had been reached on the monetary package and on the Public Commission. The Prime Minister had also given his blessing to the no-strike arbitration model. It was just a matter of reducing the agreement to writing. In fact, however, it was an excruciating experience.

Miki was still out of the country. Throughout the week we conducted meetings in Herzliya and Jerusalem. The longest lasted close to forty hours. Since the hotels were charging us only for use of the conference rooms, we probably set a world record for non-paying overnight guests. We also encountered logistic problems. We often did not know in advance where we were going to meet, how many meeting rooms we would require and for how long. Consequently, as the hotel staff needed to prepare the rooms we stayed in for other functions, we were shuffled from one room to another. On several occasions we had to conduct simultaneous sessions in odd places, such as the hotel's terrace, the lobby and behind a partition in the main dining hall.

THE LAWYERS

The beginning of the week brought new players to center stage—the lawyers. From the moment they came on the scene, the lawyers became the lead actors. Six lawyers participated in the negotiations, two each representing the Wage and Labor Agreements Division, Clalit and the IMA. One of the IMA lawyers was an outside labor lawyer. The second was the IMA in-house counsel. In addition, the head of the Department of Labor Disputes at the Ministry of Justice played an active role behind the scenes and served as liaison with the Attorney General.

The IMA had initially intended to keep its outside labor counsel in the background, relying on its in-house counsel and General Manager to represent the IMA in the drafting. The IMA leaders said that for the more difficult legal issues they would rely on my expertise in labor law. I advised the IMA to engage its own labor lawyer to look out for its interests during the negotiations over drafting language. I also explained that if either party sought my advice on labor law issues, this would put me in an untenable position.

Having its own labor counsel was the right move. It gave the IMA a great deal of confidence. It also enabled me to be neutral, utilizing my expertise in labor law to moderate the debate and to offer creative solutions when negotiations deadlocked.

When the lawyers entered the negotiation, a major problem emerged in the dynamics of the mediation. Although the lawyers were newcomers to the process, they tended to take over the discussion. They had their own ideas of how things should be done. More importantly, practically speaking, they had the power to make things go their way. Unfortunately, in the approach that they adopted, the lawyers were five weeks behind the rest of us. They had not experienced the transformative process of five weeks of highly intense mediation.

We had to move forward quickly; we could not afford to go back to day one. We decided to design the sessions, including the separate sessions, in such a way as to ensure that a member of the mediation team and representatives of the parties who had personally experienced the mediation process would always be present with the lawyers at every session. Once again, having a mediation team rather than a single mediator proved to be a major asset.

From the outset, we encountered another major problem. Although we had convened the meeting with the lawyers to work on drafting, the monetary package was, to use Zartman's terminology,[1] just a bare formula. Much work still had to be done on the details. The other two components, the Public Commission and the no-strike arbitration model, presented challenges of their own. These ideas were in the formative stage. The parties still had to give them meaning and content, and to define how they would be implemented. We suggested that we split into two groups. One group would be in charge of drafting the economic package and the collective agreement. The other group would work on the documents dealing with the Public Commission and the no-strike arbitration model.

THE ECONOMIC PACKAGE

During the mediation the parties arrived at a basic understanding of the main ingredients of the economic package. The total cost could not exceed 13.2 percent, salary increases would be on a sliding scale, interns would receive the greatest increase, the salary base for pensions and sick leave would increase from 35–40 percent to 60–70 percent of doctors' income and new doctors would be enrolled in a contributory pension plan. When the time came to reducing these understandings to writing in an actual contract, a host of legal,[2] practical and economic[3] problems arose. We had no time to work sequentially, that is, to deal with these problems first, and fine-tuning the economic package, and only then move to drafting. In order to proceed, we had to advance on both fronts simultaneously, for which purpose we formed two separate teams.

The larger team was nicknamed the "Legal Table." It included one lawyer from the Wage and Labor Agreements Division, the lawyers representing Clalit, representatives of the parties and one member of the mediation team. "Legal Table" was actually a misnomer. True, it invested much time and effort in discussing legal issues and drafting. Nevertheless, the majority of its work involved renegotiating the economic package. In addition, given the differences in legal framework and working conditions of doctors employed by the state, Clalit and Hadassah, the team also had to negotiate separate subpackages with each employer, making sure that these separate negotiated results also harmonized with the general economic package.

Representatives of the Public Service Commissioner and Clalit, as well as the IMA's experts on wage and salary administration and pensions, were active players in the Legal Table. It is noteworthy that the IMA official who at the beginning of the mediation had been extremely pessimistic about the value of mediation and later urged us not to leave, emerged as an advocate for the mediation process and the settlement. He made invaluable contributions to the discussion of the Legal Table.

During most of the Legal Table's sessions, the IMA was not represented. Its in-house counsel explained that she had full trust in the lawyers representing the Wage and Labor Agreements Division and Clalit. As a result, except in moments of crisis, the IMA lawyers worked exclusively on the documents dealing with the Public Commission and the no-strike arbitration agreement. In fact, only on the day of the closing did the IMA lawyers comment on the final draft of the collective agreement.

The smaller team was nicknamed the "Economic Table." Its composition was similar to that of the team that we had formed earlier to work on the data issue. It consisted of two representatives from the Wage and Labor Agreements Division (one of them, the Associate Director, rotated between the Legal Table and the Economic Table), three employers' representatives (from the Ministry of Health, Clalit and the Public Service Commission), a representative of the Budget Division at the Finance Ministry, the IMA's accountant and a member of the mediation team. The Economic Table's task was to analyze the data and to arrive at agreed-upon calculations regarding the cost of the agreement. This work was crucial because of the 13.2 percent ceiling.

The Economic Table's task proved to be almost insurmountable. At times it seemed that we would never be able to bring the parties to agreement. The sharp disagreement within the Economic Table was not only with respect to final results. Its members were unable to come up with an agreed-upon database and calculation procedure.

This unfortunate state of affairs could be attributed to several causes. First, the idea of costing a collective agreement was still new. Consequently, the economists could not agree on a single method for calculating costs or on the underlying assumptions. Second, the existence of four distinctive populations of doctors—those employed by the state, by Clalit and by Hadassah, as well as a fourth group of doctors working in clinics—each with its own composition and working conditions, further complicated the cost analysis. Third, the IMA had received the data on state-employed doctors relatively late in the day and had not been able to study it carefully. According to the IMA's preliminary study, the data collection and analysis were deficient. Fourth, the data regarding doctors employed by Clalit, who constituted two-thirds of the doctors represented by the IMA, was supplied only in the last days of the mediation. Consequently, all prior calculations were found to be wrong, as they were based on extrapolations from a small and entirely different population.

We never reached a fully satisfactory resolution of the issue of data supply. In retrospect, the lingering lack of trust in the data severely complicated our job. Luckily, the participants in the Economic Table developed highly cooperative working relationships. This cooperative spirit enabled them to reach consensus in the final days of the mediation on a set of principles for calculating cost and evaluating data. This set of principles permitted the members of the Economic Table to define precisely the areas of agreement and disagreement, and enabled the parties' leaders to quickly reach final resolution of the economic package.

Throughout the week there was constant discourse and exchange of information between the Legal and Economic Tables. In fact, as the terms of the economic package kept changing at the Legal Table and different results were produced by the Economic Table, the two teams continued to work in full cooperation until a final draft was completed.

THE PUBLIC COMMISSION AND THE
NO-STRIKE ARBITRATION

The negotiations over the documents dealing with the Public Commission and the no-strike arbitration model were much more complex than the negotiation over the economic package. The negotiating team, which was nicknamed the "Arbitration Team," was also different in size, make-up and structure from the two teams working on the economic package. The Arbitration Team was composed of two lawyers from the Wage and Labor Agreements Division, two lawyers representing the IMA (the in-house counsel and a labor lawyer who was also a prominent labor law professor) and myself as the mediator.

The composition of two teams negotiating the economic package (the Legal and Economic Tables) tended to be flexible; representatives of the parties felt free to observe and even to join in the negotiations. By contrast, the composition of the Arbitration Team remained unchanged[4] and its sessions were held behind closed doors. The difference might be explained by the fact that the Arbitration Team was composed of lawyers only. Their responsibility was to agree on two documents. The first dealt with the Public Commission and the second with the no-strike provisions and the arbitration procedure.

There was a substantial difference between the two documents. As the Public Commission was part of the political deal but not part of the collective agreement between the employers and the IMA, its written charter would be in the form of a letter signed by the Prime Minister. By contrast, the no-strike arbitration model would be in form of a collective agreement. Both tasks were considered purely legal. In fact they were not.

In the early stages of the mediation, we had had several discussions with the Prime Minister's office and the parties, and even exchanged drafts outlining possible parameters for the Public Commission and the no-strike arbitration. As a result of this exchange and the very nature of the two concepts, it was evident that the Public Commission was more developed, less provocative and raised no particular legal problems. By contrast, the no-strike arbitration model was still vague, legally unclear and in some sense threatening. There was only a general understanding that the agreement would be for ten years and that the arbitration board would be tripartite, composed of a neutral arbitrator, who would act as a chairman, and two partisan arbitrators representing the parties.[5] It was evident that the no-strike arbitration would be the main focus of the negotiations of the Arbitration Team.

The Public Commission

The first document, describing the Public Commission, had in fact been produced a few days earlier as a mediators' proposal. We wrote it in response to a specific request made jointly by the Prime Minister's office and the parties. Trying to come up with a mediators' proposal that would be acceptable to everyone, we had used a single text technique.[6] We sent the first draft to the IMA Chairman, the Director, and the Division of Budget at the Finance Ministry, asking for comments. The final version of the mediators' proposal was issued after two more drafts were circulated, and following discussions with the IMA in-house counsel and the senior lawyer at the Division. It was brought to our attention that neither the Government nor the Prime Minister could agree on the Public Commission without the Attorney General's approval. I asked the head of the Labor Disputes Department at the Ministry of Justice to forward our document to the Attorney General and to secure his approval.

The final document was entitled "The Commission for the Examination of Public Health Care and the Status of Doctors—A Mediators' Proposal." It discussed the need for systemic thinking regarding public health care and the status of doctors. It emphasized working conditions and working standards. It addressed major issues in the nation's ailing health care system, among which were the following:

- Redefining the concepts of public versus private health care.
- Should health care be predominately public?
- The relationship between public and private health care systems.
- Should private practice be allowed in public hospitals?
- What types of human resource management policies and practices could maintain high quality medical care and increase doctors' motivation (e.g., new forms of employment relations and compensation systems, salary structure, promotion and rotation, standards relating to private practice).

We proposed that the Public Commission would be chaired by a highly respected public figure, and composed of specialists in economics, health administration, management, medicine, human resource management and labor relations. The Commission would submit its report and non-binding recommendations within one year.

Once our document was distributed, we refused all requests to change it.[7] We insisted that the document reflected what we believed to be acceptable. As far as we were concerned, it was a mediators' proposal, a suggestion only, a starting point for further negotiations. As it turned out, we underestimated the importance of a written mediators' proposal.

Although our document was written in general terms and left several important practical issues unanswered, after hours of negotiation in the Arbitration Team the parties withdrew their demands and adopted it with only two minor modifications. One was the deletion from the definition of the general mission of the Public Commission of the emphasis on working conditions and work standards. The other was the deletion of the specific reference to salary structure and salary differentials.

The parties and the Prime Minister's office further agreed that, instead of a letter indicating the Government's decision to appoint a Public Commission, the Prime Minister would simply add his signature to the bottom of the amended mediators' proposal to signify his commitment to the appointment of the Public Commission. The fact that the IMA did not insist on a more detailed exposition was clear proof of the enormous degree of trust that had been built up during the mediation.

The No-strike Arbitration

Initially, we followed the same consensus-building technique for the no-strike arbitration document. After circulating several drafts and soliciting comments, we produced a document entitled "An Innovative Model for Contract Renewal Negotiations: Arbitration and Waiving the Right to Strike—A Mediators' Proposal."

The document described the following no-strike arbitration model:

(1) The IMA would waive the right to strike for ten years, during which time two or three agreements would be negotiated.
(2) As arbitration would replace the right to strike, scope of the strike ban would overlap the scope of subject matters that could be brought to arbitration.
(3) Arbitration could be invoked by any party at any time, but no earlier than three months after contract negotiations had begun.
(4) The arbitration would deal only with interest disputes[8] stemming from contract renewal negotiations at the national level. Right disputes would be brought to arbitration by mutual consent.
(5) The arbitration could not address government action.
(6) Disagreements regarding arbitrability would be determined by the Labor Court.
(7) The arbitration board would be tripartite[9] with a neutral arbitrator as chairman and two party appointees: the Director and the IMA Chairman.
(8) At the beginning of each round of negotiation, the parties would choose whether the arbitration would be conventional or final-offer arbitration.[10]
(9) In its decision, the arbitration board would consider the following criteria: pay and working conditions in similar occupations, the labor market for doctors, special job conditions (stress, responsibility, educational requirements, physical conditions), pay and working conditions of doctors

abroad, economic policy (including wage policy in the public sector), stability of labor relations, parity and differentials with other employee groups, ability to pay, cost of living, contribution and remuneration ratios.

(10) The arbitration award would be made within ninety days from the appointment of the board and would be regarded as a collective agreement.

(11) Any breach of the no-strike obligation would nullify the employers' obligation to submit to arbitration.

The no-strike arbitration document was more comprehensive and detailed than its counterpart dealing with the Public Commission. Its fate, however, was entirely different. When it was presented to the Arbitration Team, it is fair to say that all hell broke loose.

Even before the Arbitration Team had convened, we knew that both parties were displeased with certain aspects of our no-strike arbitration model. Both sides had expressed dissatisfaction with the proposed list of decision-making criteria for the arbitration board, and the lawyers representing the employers were unhappy with aspects of the enforceability of the no-strike obligation. Nonetheless, none of these issues were the actual reason for the unexpected outburst. Instead, it was the scope of the no-strike obligation.

At dawn, as the Arbitration Team, already exhausted from a long night of negotiations, began talking about no-strike arbitration on the hotel terrace, looking out over the Mediterranean, it dawned on the lawyers from the Wage and Labor Agreements Division that the IMA had been talking all along only of a partial waiver of its right to strike. The IMA would not strike during contract renewal negotiations, since unsettled demands would be submitted to arbitration. But the IMA intended to remain free to strike over all other issues which, under the proposed no-strike arbitration model, were not subject to mandatory arbitration.[11]

The different understandings regarding the scope of the no-strike obligation immediately ignited a heated debate, which escalated rapidly. The lawyers from the Wage and Labor Agreements Division contended that from the moment the idea of the no-strike arbitration model had first been raised by the mediators, the IMA had given the impression that in exchange for arbitration it was prepared to forgo the use of the strike weapon for a period of ten years, regardless of the reason for the strike. It was only on the basis of this understanding that the Government was willing even to consider the no-strike arbitration model. The senior lawyer from the Wage and Labor Agreements Division continued with a serious allegation. She said that the IMA had misled the Government into believing that the IMA was truly committed to the idea of strike-free labor relations. It was a breach of trust and bad faith bargaining. The Government, at any rate, would insist on no less than a ten-year sweeping waiver of the right to strike.

The IMA lawyers, on the other hand, said that the Government's understanding regarding the scope of the no-strike obligation was unfounded. It was either wishful thinking or a bargaining ploy, designed to place the IMA in a position where it was forced to reject the no-strike arbitration model entirely, thus sparing the Government the political cost of having to reject the plan itself. The IMA argued that the Government's understanding was unrealistic. No one would expect a union to give up its right to strike unless it received in exchange a strike substitute. If the Government was willing to arbitrate contract renewal disputes only, this dictated the scope of the no-strike obligation. Finally, the IMA pointed out that the document submitted by the mediators called for a limited waiver of the right to strike, in other words, only with regard to disputes that could be brought to arbitration.

I was surprised by the forcefulness with which this legitimate disagreement erupted. Although ostensibly it was over the issues of arbitrability and the scope of the strike ban, it in fact reflected a deeper fear that the parties were experiencing just before committing themselves to the proposed strategic change. It seemed that both sides undervalued their gains from the trade-off between arbitration and the right to strike and overvalued the price they were paying. The employers were unwilling to pay a high price for what the IMA regarded as a major sacrifice on its part, namely, giving up its right to strike. And the IMA was not willing to pay a high price for what the Government saw as a major sacrifice on *its* part, namely, giving up its sovereign power.

Both sides still clung to outdated and unrealistic images and perceptions. For instance, the IMA ignored the fact that with the growth of clinics, outpatient care and private medicine, the strike weapon was becoming obsolescent. Its leaders remembered the old days when a hospital strike, or even the threat of one, resulted in major economic gains. The Government, and especially the Finance Ministry, clung to the idea that arbitration could interfere with their ability to allocate the budget on a purely rational basis. They ignored the fact that strikes, especially in essential services, might interfere in this allegedly purely rational decision-making process as well.

Moreover, the Prime Minister himself had only reluctantly assented to the arbitration model. He still had to deal with resistance from the Finance Ministry and the Attorney General's office. Consequently, the Director of the Wage and Labor Agreements Division, probably the only high-ranking official who truly believed (although admittedly with certain reservations) in experimenting with the no-strike arbitration model, could not bring back to the Government anything less than a full no-strike commitment. Interestingly, the IMA leadership was experiencing a similar problem. They could not ask their membership to give up the right to strike for anything less than the Government's sweeping commitment to arbitration.

From the time we first raised the idea of no-strike arbitration and until the Arbitration Team convened, there were many hours of discussion with the parties and their constituencies. These discussions were devoted exclusively to the arbitration, not to the no-strike part of the model. While the Government side was horrified by the idea of relinquishing its power to a non-partisan arbitration board, for the IMA this aspect was the central pillar of the model. For years the IMA had been looking for ways to place its future in the hands of a neutral decision-making body instead of the Finance Ministry. It is no wonder, therefore, that both sides concentrated solely on the arbitration and paid no attention whatsoever to the no-strike aspect of the model.

In retrospect, as mediators, the fact that the parties were not discussing the no-strike obligation should not have stopped us from fully explaining it earlier. We simply could not imagine that there would be any misunderstanding, as the scope of the no-strike obligation was clearly spelled out in the mediators' proposal.

When the heated debate over the right to strike erupted, it quickly brought the Arbitration Team's negotiation to an impasse. I adjourned the session instantly. Luckily, we had to leave the hotel in any case in order to continue the sessions in Jerusalem. On the way there, just before I fell asleep in the cab, I called the Prime Minister's Chief of Staff. I reported what had happened and asked if I could come to his office with the Arbitration Team to try to save the deal. I had no choice. I had to bring an additional player into the negotiation over the no-strike arbitration, even if only temporarily. This was necessary since the mediators were in a tenuous position. After all, the crisis was over an underlying premise in our proposal. It was we who had suggested an overlap between the scope of the no-strike obligation and arbitrability. A meeting was scheduled for later that afternoon. Although there was a great deal of pessimism, we did not lose hope. We urged the Economic Team to continue its negotiations, while the Arbitration Team was waiting for the meeting at the office of the Prime Minister's Chief of Staff.

The meeting with the Chief of Staff started as a continuation of the session earlier that morning. During the short presentations the problem was again framed by the senior lawyer from the Wage and Labor Agreements Division as a complete betrayal of trust. She contended that throughout the negotiations the IMA leaders had given the Government the impression that, as far as the doctors were concerned, once the agreement was signed, the health care system would be strike-free for ten years. At the session that morning she was astonished to learn that in fact the IMA had never meant to abandon strikes entirely for ten years, merely to put them on hold during the two or three occasions on which contract renewals were negotiated. She conceded that within the Government and the inner circles of the employers, she and the Director of the Wage and Labor Agreements Division had been the strongest supporters of the no-strike arbitration model. Had she known the IMA's true intention earlier, not only would she not have given it her support, she would have actively opposed the idea.

The Chief of Staff said that he shared her understanding. For the Government, the proposal's appeal was the opportunity to prevent doctors' strikes without legislation. It was to that end that the Government was ready to relinquish its ultimate decision-making power and submit to arbitration.

This was the most disturbing moment of the mediation. We were close to reaching agreement on the economic package and had agreed on the Public Commission. The dispute over the scope of the strike ban was a setback that threatened to destroy the whole deal. It had also become a strategic issue and a clear deal-breaker with no room for compromise. We had to dig deeper to find a solution. I suggested that we move to private caucuses, and asked the IMA lawyers to wait in an adjacent room.

I told the Chief of Staff and the lawyers from the Wage and Labor Agreements Division that I understood their need for a full strike ban. The Government perceived no-strike arbitration as a new model of labor relations. To that end, nothing less than a strike-free environment would suffice. Nonetheless, to convince the IMA to accept a broad strike ban we would have to find a way to address the IMA's underlying needs. We would need to find a way to maintain the IMA's bargaining power for non-contract negotiation disputes in the absence of the ability to strike.

I then explained to the IMA attorneys that we understood their thinking. Nonetheless, given the Government's need for a simple strike-free model, they had no choice but to acquiesce to a full strike ban. I suggested that they identify particular areas where a full strike ban might harm the IMA's interests. This exercise might help our search for pragmatic solutions that could accommodate the IMA's needs, while leaving the full strike ban intact.

This course of action was something both sides could live with. The IMA agreed in principle to a ten-year full strike ban, provided the agreement did not leave the doctors completely powerless in situations that were not covered by the contract renewal arbitration. In response, the lawyers from the Wage and Labor Agreements Division declared that the Government had never intended to use the strike ban to gain any advantage. They were willing to work together with the IMA to find creative measures to protect the IMA's interests without a strike. The crisis was over, at least for now.

This agreement marked the beginning of a long and difficult search for a strike substitute. The process included mapping out types of foreseeable disputes, and for each one, identifying a mutually acceptable dispute resolution procedure. As a result of these joint efforts, not only were we able to finally break the deadlock, but we also reached a more elaborate and comprehensive agreement.

First, the parties agreed to a sweeping waiver of the right to strike for ten years. Second, the mediators' proposal was appended to the agreement with the stipulation that it would be applicable only in disputes over contract renewals. Third, a separate arbitration procedure under the general Law of Arbitration of 1985 was instituted for specific mid-term disputes. Fourth, all other disputes would be referred for resolution either to a third type of arbitration procedure available under the Settlement of Labor Disputes Law of 1957[12] or to the Labor Court.

The task of negotiating an acceptable system of dispute resolution to replace the strike was time-consuming. When it was over, the Arbitration Team had completed just one part of its task. There was still the arbitration model to design. The parties' demands had not yet been addressed. To make things worse, there were new design issues stemming from the fact that the parties had agreed that future disputes would be resolved through three different arbitration procedures. These were the special tripartite arbitration board for contract renewal negotiation, the conventional arbitration mechanism under the Law of Arbitration of 1965 and the statutory arbitration mechanism under the Settlement of Labor Disputes Law of 1957.

On the morning of the final day, the Arbitration Team was under severe time pressure. It had completed twenty-four hours of marathon sessions. The teams working on the economic package were in last phase of fine-tuning their draft. There was no apparent reason to extend the negotiations and the strike until all these design issues could be resolved. We suggested that the Arbitration Team continue its joint efforts to resolve the most important issues and leave the reminder for post-agreement negotiations. The parties embraced this idea. The agreement to leave these design issues for post-agreement negotiation was based on the trust which had been built during the joint search for different dispute processing procedures which would function as strike substitutes during the term of the agreement.

They agreed on extending to six months the length of time before arbitration could be invoked. In addition, at the request of the Director of the Wage and Labor Agreements Division, the IMA agreed to omit from the list of decision-making criteria the following two criteria: comparison with pay and working conditions of doctors abroad and the "output income ratio". Finally, the parties wrote a preliminary draft appendix of detailed timetables and methods of arbitrator selection for the various arbitration procedures. It was agreed that a final version of the appendix would be signed within thirty days.[13] Everything was ready for final drafting and closing.

During the final days I felt like an orchestra conductor who is also the featured soloist. I had to oversee, and at times actively participate in, the negotiations of the Legal and the Economic Tables, which were largely run by the assistant mediators. In addition, I mediated the most difficult negotiations of the Arbitration Team.

As if to be involved as mediator in three negotiation tables was not enough, I was forced to preside over a fourth negotiation. This was a last-minute sidetable mediation with a group called the Interns Association. This is the subject of the next chapter.

NOTES

1. William I. Zartman & Maureen R. Bernan, *The Practical Negotiator* 87–146 (1982).

2. For instance, we learned that in the case of state-employed doctors, it would be impossible to increase the salary base for pension purposes without passing appropriate legislation.

3. For instance, according to several simulations run by the Wage and Labor Agreements Division, the costs of implementing the whole package would exceed the 13.2% ceiling.

4. On several occasions, especially at moments of crisis, the team was joined by the Director of the Wage and Labor Agreements Division and the IMA Chairman.

5. This unique composition seems to work well in arbitration of interest disputes. See Thomas A. Kochan, Mordehai Mironi, Ronald G. Ehrenberg, Jean Baderschneider & Todd Jick, *Dispute Resolution under Factfinding and Arbitration: An Empirical Analysis* 96–105 (1978).

6. On single text, see: Saadia Touval, "Multilateral Negotiation: An Analytic Approach" 5 Neg. J. 159 (1989); Paul W. Thurner & Franz Urban Pappi, "Domestic and International Politics During an EU Intergovernmental Conference: Bridging the Gap between Negotiation Theory and Practice" 22 *Neg. J* 167 (2006).

7. For instance, responding to a concern of the Finance Ministry, the Prime Minister's office asked to add to our document a statement that, in deciding whether to adopt the Public Commission's recommendations, the Prime Minister would consider income and economic policies.

8. On the distinction between interest and right disputes see *supra*, note 1. ch. 10.

9. See text preceding , note 5, *supra*.

10. On final offer arbitration, its history virtues and pitfalls, see: James L. Stern, Charles M. Rehmus, Joseph Loewenberg, Hirschel Kaspar, Barbara D. Dennis, *Final*

Offer Arbitration (1975); Arnold Zack, "Final Offer Selection—Panacea or Pandora Box" 19 N.Y. L. F. 567 (1974); John G. Treble, "How New is Final-Offer Arbitration" 25 *Indus. Rel.* 92 (1986).

11. In Israel, strikes during the term of the collective agreement are a common phenomenon.

12. Section 37E of the Settlement of Labor Disputes Law.

13. Four months after the agreement was signed, I was asked by the parties to assist them to reach agreement on the design issues. We were able to resolve these issues in one meeting.

Chapter Fourteen

Last-Minute Side-Table Mediation—The Interns

Back in the first week of mediation, the IMA had presented a long list of demands. One concerned the working hours of interns. The issue of overworked interns is not unique to Israeli hospitals. We learned that many prior attempts in various countries to solve this problem had failed.

Generally speaking, interns were assigned the vast majority of on-duty shifts in the hospitals, often outside their formally assigned departments, typically in emergency rooms and intensive care units. Usually the shift would start in the late afternoon at the end of the regular working day, and end the following morning. By then, the intern had been working for twenty-four hours. In the morning, instead of leaving the hospital, he (or she) would be asked to perform his (or her) regular duties in his (or her) own department, sometimes for another full working day. We also learned that the 1976 and 1994 collective agreements gave the interns up to 25 days of paid leave to study for their qualifying exams to compensate them for the days they worked following on-duty shifts.

The IMA wanted the practice of interns working after on-duty shifts to cease, and added it as an item for negotiation. In contrast to other IMA demands, this one caused no disagreement around the table. To the contrary, everyone agreed that the practice had been a problem for years. In addition, it had negative consequences for the quality of health care being provided to the public, as well as for the interns' own health, safety,[1] quality of professional life and personal and family life. The representatives of the Ministry of Health shared with us their own frustration regarding repeated attempts to solve or at least alleviate the problem, all of which had been unsuccessful.

The issue of interns working after on-duty shifts was discussed briefly two or three times during the first two weeks of the mediation. Reference was also made in passing to a case that dealt with the issue and was pending in the Supreme Court.

As is commonly the case in collective contract negotiations, only a small fraction of the issues on the parties' lists of demands made it to the advanced, let alone the final stages of negotiation. The issue of interns' work after on-duty shifts was one such issue that fell by the wayside. It had been raised at the initial stage of negotiations and had been recognized as an important and integrative issue. Nonetheless, at later stages it disappeared from the negotiation table along with many other issues.

Towards the end of the fifth week, about ten days before closing, the issue of interns' work after on-duty shifts erupted with irresistible force and from an unexpected direction—the Supreme Court. I was handed a copy of an interim restraining order enjoining the Finance Ministry from signing any agreement with the IMA. The restraining order had actually been issued by the Supreme Court[2] on December 1999, six months before the mediation begun. It was issued in a case filed by the Interns Association against the Minister of Labor and the Finance Minister concerning the practice of interns' work after on-duty shifts.[3] For reasons that remained unknown to us, the parties had not shared this information with the mediation team up until this point.

When we first heard of the restraining order, the parties in the mediation were already making the final steps towards settlement. The restraining order now hung over our heads and it was in danger of becoming an insurmountable barrier to signing an agreement and ending the strike. We were puzzled by the fact that the parties had not shared this information with us earlier. but instead of discussing this question, we asked the parties how they were going to cope with the restraining order if they reached agreement. The parties suggested several creative solutions: signing the agreement but not registering it,[4] or initialing a letter of understanding accompanied by a draft agreement and depositing it with me as trustee. Unfortunately, none of these ideas complied with the sweeping nature of the restraining order.

I spoke with the Head of the Department of Labor Disputes at the Ministry of Justice, who was representing the two Ministries in the proceedings before the Supreme Court. I asked her to petition the court to request a stay or other summary relief that would enable the parties to sign the agreement. When no progress was made, I called the Attorney General to explain to him the urgency of the situation. I also called and faxed the Prime Minister's Chief of Staff and the Government Secretary in an effort to enlist their assistance in convincing the Attorney General to act.

Days passed by and all my efforts to motivate the Attorney General and the Ministry of Justice to take action in the matter were in vain. It was time to change track.

I called the lawyer representing the Interns Association. I suggested that the Interns Association should join the negotiations and try to resolve the issue of interns' work after on-duty shifts through the mediation rather than through the courts. After a brief consultation with the leadership of the interns, she agreed.

We brought the idea to the parties. It was a delicate situation. After all, the Interns Association was a splinter union, representing only a minority of the interns, and thus in certain respects an "illegitimate player." All interns were IMA members, but this group had opted for separate representation and an independent course of action. Letting the Interns Association join the negotiation as a full-fledged party meant granting them legitimacy. It might lead to a rift within the IMA and to future claims by the interns to be recognized in negotiations as a separate bargaining unit . Neither the IMA nor the employers could afford to let this happen.[4]

We had to find a way to engage the Interns Association in the talks without making them formally a party to the negotiations and the agreement. We suggested that the talks with the interns be conducted as a side-table negotiation under the auspices of the mediation team. The parties agreed. They recognized that there was no other practical way to circumvent the restraining order, and the idea of side-table negotiations carried no risk. We asked the Ministry of Health, Clalit and the Director of the Wage and Labor Agreements Division to send delegates to the meeting with the Interns Association.

And so it happened that four days before the parties concluded the agreement, while the mediation team was busy working at three negotiation tables, a fourth side-table was added. Having already appropriated all free conference rooms in the hotel, the meeting with the Interns Association leadership[6] and their legal counsel was held in the hotel's business lounge, which was full of guests.

In spite of the time pressures, we did not take any shortcuts. We began with an introduction to mediation. We then explained that whatever would be agreed upon in the mediation with the interns would be brought by the mediators to the negotiating parties, i.e., to the Director, the IMA and the employers. If approved, it would be incorporated into the collective agreement.

It appeared that the interns preferred to reach agreement rather than fight their case in court. Consequently, the two delegations taking part in the interns' mediation agreed quickly to a model for a solution aimed at eliminating interns' work after on-duty shifts. The model included the following elements: (1) strict limits on the type of duties and number of hours an intern could be asked to work after completing an on-duty shift; (2) enforcement of these limits through disciplinary action, if necessary; (3) special monitoring, reporting and disciplinary procedures in every hospital, under close supervision of the Ministry of Health; and (4) the granting of special study leave, unrelated to the number of hours worked after on-duty shifts. It was further agreed that one chapter of the collective agreement that was to be signed by the IMA and the employers would be devoted to the subject of interns' work after on-duty shifts. The Interns Association's counsel would take part in drafting this chapter.

After the mediation with the Interns' Association, direct communication with its counsel continued over the next three days, as several drafts of the relevant chapter of the collective agreement were emailed back and forth and numerous telephone conversations were held. The process continued until the model for the solution finally took shape, and the counsel agreed to the contract language. Since implementing the model required amending the applicable legislation, she asked for an undertaking to this effect signed by the General Manager of the Ministry of Health.

Following the conclusion of the side-mediation with the Interns' Association, I was now confident that we could proceed to signing the agreements. The Interns Association's counsel had promised to send a letter stating that the Interns' Association would petition the High Court of Justice to withdraw its restraining order and the Interns Association's petition, and stating also that it had no objection to the Finance Ministry signing the agreements with the IMA in spite of the restraining order which had been issued at its request. Relying on this letter rather than waiting for the High Court of Justice to act was a calculated risk that the parties and the mediation team were willing to take.

At noon on the last day of the mediation, the final drafts of the three documents, namely the new collective agreement, the mandate for the Public Commission and the no-strike arbitration agreement were at last ready.

We arranged a meeting with the General Manager of the Ministry of Health and the Prime Minister's Chief of Staff to ascertain that the General Manager was committed to the changes to the legislation that had been agreed with the interns.[7] Then, just two hours before the scheduled time for the signing ceremony, I received the formal letter from the Interns Association's counsel. The letter removed the last obstacle to signing the agreements. At last, we were done.

NOTES

1. There is a case that is well-known among medical professionals in Israel of an intern who was killed in a car accident as a result of falling asleep while driving home after thirty consecutive hours of work at the hospital.

2. Sitting as the High Court of Justice. Under Israeli law, actions taken by the Government and other public entities such as municipalities and statutory agencies are subject to judicial review by the High Court of Justice. The Supreme Court and the High Court of Justice have a common bench. The former hears civil and criminal appeals, while the latter sits as a court of first impression.

3. H.C.J. 6576/99, *Interns Association v. Minister of Labor and Welfare and Finance Minister*. A father whose daughter died in childbirth joined the case against the Ministry of Labor, alleging that intern fatigue was a cause of the tragedy.

4. Under the Collective Agreements Law of 1957, all collective agreements must be reduced to writing and registered with the Officer of Labor Relations at the Ministry of Labor.

5. The IMA faced an additional difficulty. As a professional association led by senior doctors and departmental heads, it had to bear in mind that any acceptable solution to the problem of the interns' working hours would necessarily come at the expense of the majority of its members.

6. Throughout the talks with the Interns Association I did not fully understand the nature of this organization and how its leadership had been selected. Due to the urgency of the situation I had neither the time nor the need to find out. I merely ascertained that the leadership had the authority to reach an agreement, and that the Interns' Association legal counsel had the requisite power of attorney to apply to the High Court of Justice asking it to withdraw the petition that had brought about the temporary injunction.

7. It subsequently emerged that the agreement with the interns caused many budgeting and operational problems for the hospitals, and therefore was only partially implemented.

Chapter Fifteen

The Grand Finale—Signing
the Agreement

Our spokesperson and the public relations officer at the Finance Ministry arranged the signing ceremony. The lawyers representing the parties joined forces to prepare the final sets of documents. While waiting for the ceremony, the mediation team met for the last time to list the main points that needed to be highlighted at the ceremony. After all, throughout the six weeks of mediation, the team's voice was never heard in public. Save for the parties' joint press releases, issued by our spokesperson, the mediation had been conducted under a strict media blackout.

The ceremony took place in a large hall packed with reporters representing virtually all the newspapers, radio and television stations in Israel. Everyone who participated in the mediation was present. I was sad that Miki, who was on a business trip in Europe, could not share this uplifting experience. On the podium were the IMA Chairman, the Director of the Wage and Labor Agreements Division, the Prime Minister's Chief of Staff, the Cabinet Secretary and I.

Each person was given five minutes to speak. I gave the opening remarks. I said that the agreement was the triumph of optimism. After two and a half years, 900 days of negotiation, 127 days of the strike and 42 days of mediation the parties had reached agreement.

Referring to the document, I said that for many in need of medical care, the fact that agreement was reached would mean the end of the strike and of their suffering. For the public at large and the medical community, the settlement would bring hope for a better future. This was because the parties were able to successfully create an innovative and revolutionary settlement, one that had the potential of improving the quality of health care by transforming working conditions and labor relations of doctors in the public health system.

The documents, which would shortly be signed, represented the parties' joint attempt to courageously deal with systemic and strategic problems that had developed and increased in complexity over many years.

The settlement comprised three elements, each addressing a different time-frame. The first was short-term: the collective agreement. Its underlying goal was not only to improve doctors' income, but also to address the long-standing problems of doctors' pensions, the convoluted salary structure and interns' working hours. In return, new doctors entering into state-employment would be transferred from a budgetary to a contributory pension plan. The second component addressed the middle range. This was the Public Commission which would be appointed by the Prime Minister and whose remit was to study the public health care system and the status of doctors from a systemic approach, and make recommendations for future action. The third and most daring component was long-range. This was the agreement under which the IMA would give up its power to strike for the next ten years. In return, the Government and other public health employers would give up their decision-making power regarding doctors' remuneration and working conditions. As a result, there would be no doctors' strikes and reason would replace force as the arbiter.

I congratulated the participants in the mediation for their contribution. This was *their* achievement. I thanked the Prime Minister and the parties for having placed their trust in the mediation process and in us. I also thanked Miki, the assistant mediators and our spokesperson. Finally, I apologized to the reporters for our spokesperson's outstanding success in keeping our work out of the media's reach.

I concluded my short address by declaring that in a few hours we would wake up to a new and better day for hospitals and clinics. I added that signing the agreement honored the people who need medical care in the future, the doctors, the employers, labor relations practitioners, the mediation community and Israeli society as a whole. This was actually the first time in the fifty-two years of Israel's history that a dispute of this magnitude,[1] one moreover in which the Government was a principal party, was settled through private mediation. Furthermore, it was the first time that a union had given up its right to strike, creating a sheltered, non-violent, strike-free environment for the sick, for the doctors and for the employers.

The parties to the agreement were about to embark on an experiment in a completely new style of labor relations. If this pilot project succeeded, not only might it be extended to other essential services, but it could change forever the culture of labor negotiations in Israel. Finally, the fact that the parties were able to settle their dispute and find an integrative solution attested to the value of mediation. If, as a result of this success, mediation were to be used to resolve similar disputes, it would benefit society at large. In the long run, it might change the disputational culture by improving the way disagreements and disputes between individuals and groups are dealt with and resolved.

All the speakers praised the agreement and the contribution of the mediation process. As one might expect, the new no-strike arbitration model drew most of the attention.

When the speakers concluded, the IMA Chairman and the Director of the Wage and Labor Agreements Division signed the collective agreement. The Prime Minister's Chief of Staff and the Cabinet Secretary signed the document dealing with the Public Commission. With perfect timing, the Prime Minister called from Camp David and congratulated the parties.

Close to forty hours after I left home, I was driving back to Tel Aviv. The end of the doctors' strike was the lead story on the radio. I felt great.

NOTE

1. The cost of the agreement were estimated by the Finance Ministry to be over $100,000,000 per year. This figure relates only to monetary costs.

Chapter Sixteen

Concluding Insights, Notes and Discussion

The case study tells it all. The story and what one can read between lines carry many lessons. Whether the reader is a negotiator, mediator, academic, policy maker, lawyer or labor relations practitioner, there are lessons and insights for all. Nevertheless, this case study would be incomplete if I did not share what I learned from the experience. Therefore, in this chapter I will highlight and briefly discuss a few important lessons that I drew from this mediation process. Some of the lessons are research-oriented, others directed at practice.

A WORD ABOUT THE TYPOLOGY OF DISPUTES

Mediating a nationwide doctors' strike is not a run-of-the-mill mediation. The voluminous ADR, employment, and labor law literature provides many typologies to classify disputes using characteristics such as the number of parties, the subject matter, the context, the relationship between the disputing parties, and so on. The doctors' strike defied simple classification. First, it combined many types of disputes. It was multi-party and multi-layered. It was a multi-issue dispute involving medical care, public policy, government, employment and labor law, labor relations, public sector labor relations and essential services. It was both inter-organizational and intra-organizational. Furthermore, the doctors' strike possessed many important properties which are not present in common typologies, among them its high level of visibility, its urgency and intensity, the heterogeneity of the parties on both sides, the intricate relationships between players both institutionally and personally, the high stakes involved and the wide scope of the direct and indirect impact of potential outcomes.

For these reasons, disputes such as the doctors' strike should be defined as a separate category: mega-disputes.

RESEARCH AND DATA COLLECTION

Writing about the dynamics of any mediation is a tricky task. This is especially true when describing and analyzing the mediation of a mega-dispute, all the more so when the writer is himself both a participant-observer and a central player in the process. In mediation, the most important (and often the sole) source of information is the mediator's notes. I tend to write extensively during mediation. The experience in the doctors' mediation led me to the following observation: *there is an inverse relation between the importance of events and the ability to take notes.*

My colleagues and I made many pages of detailed notes during the first week of the mediation and almost none during the last. The number, the intensity, and the speed of the events, which often occurred simultaneously in different locations, did not allow for the time or provide the conditions for note-taking.

THE MEDIATOR'S COMMITMENT

Given the importance of medical care, there was extreme urgency; resolving the dispute and bringing the strike to an end was a top priority. To that end, we had to be ready to invest the time needed to meet with any person at any time and at any place, irregular hours and long meetings. In addition, because of the parties' heterogeneity, the large size of the delegations and the number of people who were involved in the dispute without actually attending the mediation sessions, many hours were invested in off-session communications, either in person or over the telephone.

Some of these conversations were with the leaders of the parties or with other participants in the mediation sessions. They often needed to say things that they felt they could not voice in the sessions, not even in a caucus, or to share thoughts and ideas for the next meeting. Additional time was spent on communicating with the large group of people who were involved in the dispute but who were not part of the negotiation teams. Among these were the staff of the Prime Minister's office, various Ministers, public officials, interested doctors and others, such as family members of individuals in need of urgent medical care.

Finally, given the fact that we were a four-person mediation team, substantial time was invested in private conversations for debriefing and planning.

The understandably endless demands on our time and attention taught us an important lesson. Mediating a mega-dispute such as the doctors' strike requires total personal commitment. For us it meant that for six weeks we put aside all prior engagements and other obligations, as well as our personal lives.[1] With few exceptions,[2] we were available twenty-four hours a day, seven days a week.[3]

WHO GETS TO SIT AT THE TABLE?

In a dispute with a high degree of urgency, intensity and visibility, there is always tension as to whom to invite to participate. This is especially true when the parties have large delegations, which in turn represent multiple and heterogeneous constituencies. The problem also tends to increase in complexity with the passage of time, as pressure mounts to end the strike and leaders are called upon to make tough decisions and engage in delicate trade-offs.

For the sake of efficiency, however, it is precisely at such moments that mediation sessions need to be conducted with the smallest number of participants possible. At the same time, such meetings (which may last for many hours) can alienate members of the delegations who are left out. This need also runs counter to the idea that all the participants should undergo the transformative proceed.

The doctors' mediation carried several lessons. First, that it is not enough to inform the participants at the beginning of the mediation of the possibility of forming small meetings, even when you get all the participants to agree to it in principle in advance. The mediators need to be sensitive to the difficulties experienced by those who are not invited. They have to constantly explain to the full delegations the need for such meetings and reinforce their acceptance of them. Second, mediators need to be aware of the fact that opting for closed meetings with the parties' leaders will often place the mediators in the delicate position of having to decide who will participate and who will not. If not done with prudence and sensitivity, this may undermine the trust that exists in the mediators and their credibility. Third, it is crucial to keep all participants informed, and to conduct frequent meetings with the full delegations. Such meetings may serve to elicit their input and to ensure their acceptance both of the process and of the direction in which the resolution of the dispute is evolving.

THE MEDIATION TEAM

Mediating a mega-dispute the size of the doctors' strike calls for team mediation. Having more than one mediator on board carries several advantages over a single mediator or even co-mediation. First, since the assignment may come unexpectedly and the duration of the mediation is unforeseeable, it is difficult to clear all calendars of all prior engagements. The busier the person appointed, the more problematic it gets. A multi-member mediation team enables the sessions to continue in the absence of one or more members.[4]

Second, a multi-member team makes possible a multidisciplinary or more synergetic composition. The make-up of the team in the doctors' mediation was an important asset. It included one leading businessman and two experienced professional mediators who were lawyers, one of whom specialized in labor law and labor relations. The fourth team member was a mediator with a strong background in economics and data analysis. I cannot overstate the importance of Miki's stature as a businessman in our dealings with the Government, or of our economist's contribution in presiding over the Economic Table.[5]

Third, we listened to every person who expressed interest in the dispute and in talking to us. In every mediation that I am involved in, I continuously work on building what I call the "friendship league" of the agreement—a coalition of participants who have a higher commitment to collaborate in search of common ground, and who will lend the strongest support to the final agreement. This practice is especially important in a multi-party dispute involving heterogeneous groups. Jonathan, a member of our team and a very experienced and effective mediator, did most of the work in this regard. In any event, our multi-member team enabled us to divide among us the huge and time-consuming (albeit important) task of conducting these private conversations.

Fourth, the value of having a multi-member team was especially evident during the final week when we conducted three mediation sessions simultaneously. In fact, when the need for a fourth session arose (the side-table mediation with the Interns' Association), having only three members of the team available created a serious problem.

MEDIA COVERAGE

In recent years, Israel has witnessed a sharp increase in media coverage of labor disputes. Unions and management alike tend to engage public relations firms and media consultants as important players on their teams. One possible explanation is the low level of public tolerance towards strikes and strikers, as well as the declining utility and efficacy of the strike as a moving force in labor-management negotiations. In a high-profile dispute such as the nationwide doctors' strike, a mediator cannot afford to overlook the role of the media. The choice between fully-transparent "sunshine" negotiations and a media blackout is rather difficult. Transparency was important, since the dispute was over the allocation of public resources. On the other hand, a media blackout was perceived by us as being instrumental in speeding up the mediation and bringing the strike to a rapid close. After raising the issue with the parties, the consideration of the urgency of the situation prevailed, and the media blackout was unanimously chosen as the appropriate course of action. The understanding was that the parties could continue to talk with reporters about the dispute and about the strike, but not about the mediation. In retrospect, conducting the mediation privately was highly conducive to success.

The problem with a media blackout is how to police it and how to satisfy the media's thirst for information. Having a public relations expert as part of the mediation team was the perfect solution. She was in daily contact with the media and the parties' public relations staff. This enabled her to scout in advance any attempt to circumvent the rule. The continuing flow of free information about the strike, together with the daily joint press releases, served several purposes. First, they helped to ensure the confidentiality of the proceedings and to maintain the media blackout by appeasing the media. Second, they had the function of countering rumors and keeping the various constituencies and the public informed about the efforts of the parties to resolve the strike, and prepared the constituencies to assent to the mediated agreement.

Finally, the daily joint press releases were valuable also in terms of the process. Starting from day one, the parties entered into a daily routine of making at least one small agreement each day, namely, agreeing over the wording of the joint press release. Given the parties' failure to reach any agreement during the preceding two years of negotiations, the repeated daily success of arriving at agreed-upon texts on the progress of the negotiations was in itself a major achievement. It enhanced the negotiating teams' belief in the prospects of reaching a final agreement on the substantive issues.

THE PRIME MINISTER'S INVOLVEMENT

It needs to be emphasized that in every prolonged mega-dispute in an essential service, it is only natural to expect the head of state or chief executives to intervene in one way or another. Nonetheless, the role that the Prime Minister and his office played throughout the mediation process in the nationwide doctors' strike was probably the most irritating issue for public officials. Although the title of this section refers to the Prime Minister specifically, the questions raised refer to a wider circle and not only to the Prime Minister. It includes other officials in the Prime Minster's office, such as the Chief of Staff and the Cabinet Secretary.

To this day it remains unclear who first suggested the idea of using mediation to resolve the doctors' strike. What we do know is that the mediation was initiated by and conducted under the auspices of the Prime Minister. He and members of his office were the moving force behind the negotiations. The Prime Minister met with the mediators twice. His Chief of Staff and the Cabinet Secretary closely followed the mediation and participated actively in some of them. At the signing ceremony they sat with me on the podium.

The involvement of the Prime Minister's office in the mediation raises two related questions: Is it legitimate for the mediator to bypass the negotiation table and independently involve higher levels of decision-making, such as the Prime Minister? When the Prime Minister's office is involved, can mediation still be regarded as a voluntary process?

The Prime Minister and the Mediators

The first question addresses the problem of multilateral negotiations, which is as old as public sector collective bargaining itself.[6] It refers to the negotiation tactic in which public sector unions go over the heads of management negotiators and try to reach top officials such as the local mayor or the governor to improve their gains. The IMA is no different from other public sector unions, except that, for the IMA, reaching the Prime Minister was the strategy under which it entered the negotiations to begin with. When the IMA prolonged the strike, the expectation was that the Prime Minister would either take over the negotiations or intervene indirectly. It was evident that the Finance Ministry with its strict wage policy could not yield to the IMA's demands. The Director, the chief negotiator across the table, resisted any IMA attempt to approach the Prime Minister and his staff without going through his office.

Under these circumstances, the only question was whether mediation initiated by, and conducted under the auspices of, the Prime Minister could be used by the union to advance its multilateral negotiation strategy and achieve a better result in the negotiation.

With the exception of a single meeting between the Prime Minister and IMA's leader, Dr. Blashar, the mediation process gave the IMA only limited and indirect access to the Prime Minister. During the mediation, the mediators arranged several meetings between the IMA and officials in the Prime Minister's office. Nonetheless, except for the 0.2% the Prime Minister added to the economic settlement just before leaving for Camp David, these meetings did not affect the economic terms of the outcome. They did, however, have an impact on the mediation process and the mediators.

The relationship between the mediators and the Prime Minister, as well as the meetings arranged for the IMA by the mediators, were perceived by the

Director and other employers' representatives as a threat. Throughout the mediation they feared that the mediators would arrange a back-door deal between the IMA and the Prime Minister.

This fear was unwarranted. We made sure that the direct line of communication between the IMA and the Prime Minister's office never undermined the authority of the Director. In addition, the Prime Minister and his staff insisted that the economic package was the exclusive domain of the Director. The fact that we knew that the threat of a back-door deal was baseless did not change the Director's perception of the matter (and that of the other employers as well). As a result, the Director and the employers' representatives had, on one hand, full confidence in the neutrality of the mediators in the negotiations with the IMA. But on the other hand, they did not have complete trust in the process because of what they perceived as too close a relationship between the mediators and the Prime Minister.

At the end of the day, this ambivalence probably did not affect the doctors' mediation. However, it may have had long-term negative impact on public officials' willingness to use mediation in the future. Sometimes I wonder whether investing more time and effort throughout the negotiations in teaching these officials about the mediation process and the nature of our discussions with the Prime Minister might have alleviated this problem.

The independent relationship between the mediators and the Prime Minister and his staff had no impact on the economic deal. At the same time, the discourse between the mediators and the Prime Minister and his staff was instrumental in reaching a final settlement. After all, it was the Prime Minister who decided that the Government would accept the Public Commission and the arbitration.

Creating the Public Commission and agreeing to submit to outside arbitration are exactly the strategic choices that are exclusively for the government to make. In addition, these decisions were not taken without the concurrence of the Finance Minister and the Director. The Prime Minister made the final decision after a full debate in which all affected Ministers and public officials, as well as the mediators, were heard.

Is Mediation Voluntary?

In a conference that took place shortly after the doctors' strike, public officials complained that the basic premise of voluntarism was absent from the doctors' mediation. They explained that the Prime Minister compelled them to enter mediation. In addition, during the mediation they had the feeling that they were not free to walk out.

This is a serious concern, not only for public officials but also for mediators and the mediation process. When mediation is initiated by the Prime Minister and is conducted under his auspices, there is probably no solution to this problem. Practically speaking, the mediators should be sensitive to the problem and raise it with the negotiators. Conceptually, depending on how one defines the parties, the premise of voluntarism does exist. The party to a mega-dispute such as the doctors' strike is the state or the Government. It is the state's will that counts, not the will of its representatives, be they Ministers or high-level officials. Hence, it is the state that decides voluntarily to enter into and to continue in mediation.

SUBJECT MATTER EXPERTISE

Another lesson that can be drawn from the doctors' mediation is that familiarity with the issues on the negotiation table is always important. Here, the economic background of two of the members of our team and their ability to moderate the highly sophisticated discussions regarding alternative methods of analyzing data and costs as well as actuarial computations, were of great help. In addition, when the mediation aspires to enlarge (rather than merely to divide) the pie[7] by searching for value-creating interest-based solutions, subject matter expertise is helpful.

The fact that I am a professor of labor law with a special interest in ADR, especially dispute resolution procedures for essential employees,[8] played an important role in the doctors' mediation. It enabled me to contribute to the educational process that led the Government to adopt the no-strike arbitration model. It was also useful during the final week's negotiations in the Arbitration Team. The way in which we were finally able to resolve the crisis over the scope of the strike ban was a perfect exercise in dispute process design.[9]

But having relevant subject matter expertise can have a downside. A mediator should not have a stake in the outcome. At times I realized that this was not true in the doctors' mediation. For years I have held a strong belief in the idea of arbitration as a strike substitute for essential employees. It might well be that I had a stake in leading the parties to embrace this idea. Fortunately the IMA's counsel was also a professor of labor law, one whom I knew and respected, and she had previously been engaged in research on interest arbitration.[10] I assume that it was her work with the IMA's leaders and activist members that made the IMA so receptive to the innovative idea of no-strike arbitration model.

THE LAWYERS

A lot can be written about the role of lawyers in the doctors' mediation. This section will deal just with one question that is often raised in mediation: when is the right time to involve the lawyers? The question is particularly relevant in a prolonged negotiation, where the parties attempt first to agree on a deal and then to submit it to the lawyers for drafting.

The doctors' mediation is a good context in which to examine this question. The mediation lasted for a relatively long period, the terms of settlement were complicated and had far reaching consequences, and there were immense legal problems. The mediated solution in the doctors' strike represented a considerable challenge for the lawyers. To begin with, the legal framework of the contractual relationship was complicated. The collective agreement was a multi-employer nationwide agreement that had to be applied to highly diversified population of doctors. The final deal only added complex legal problems, including drafting the contractual and statutory changes needed to effectuate the increase in base salaries for pensions, designing and writing special disciplinary procedures for the enforcement of the ban on interns working after on-duty shifts (including the necessary changes to the law) and designing and drafting the unique ten-year agreement regarding the no-strike and arbitration procedures. Nonetheless, the lawyers were brought in only in the final week.

Throughout the drafting week we experienced enormous pressure and went through a major crisis that threatened to shatter the tentative terms of settlement. In spite of all this, I am convinced that the parties made the right decision in bringing the lawyers in at the end of the mediation. It was probably good for them, and it also benefited the mediation process.

During the first weeks of mediation we were trying to create a new discourse among the players in their day-to-day labor relations and at the same time to develop an interest-based dialogue for the future. There was no room for the lawyers since, by definition, they were only sporadic visitors to the public health care environment. There was also the risk that the lawyers might dominate the discussion, leaving very little room for the members of the negotiating teams to participate in a meaningful dialogue. Finally, there was the fear that, due to their profession, the lawyers might affect the nature of the discourse with their rights-based philosophical map.[11]

Before concluding, three additional comments should be made. First, I see a distinction between the role of lawyers in mediation of contractual negotiations, sometimes referred to as deal-making negotiation or interest dispute,[12] and in mediation of right disputes or settlement negotiation, where mediation is used to assist the parties to reach an out-of-court settlement. The mediation in the doctors' strike was of the former type—a contract renewal negotiation. In this type of negotiation, early intervention by lawyers in the mediation is less important. Second, lawyers can be creative and may help their clients identify and clarify their interests. Legal representation can be an important empowering device in negotiations. Had the parties wanted to involve their lawyers at an earlier stage we would not have objected. Third, when lawyers enter at the end of a long mediation process, one should expect a temporary and sometimes risky backsliding. The doctors' mediation was a good example of this phenomenon. Several reasons may account for it. The lawyers had not undergone the transformative process during the first five weeks. In addition, they lacked a sense of ownership of the tentative agreement—a creation in which they had no part. Finally, certain aspects of the tentative agreement had to be renegotiated, since in the absence of lawyers the parties had agreed on terms that were legally unfeasible and had overlooked major legal problems.

THE MEDIATORS' PROPOSAL

The doctors' mediation may add insight to the debate as to whether mediators should provide the parties with a mediators' proposal. I am proponent of the view that the process and the solution belong to the parties, and that mediators' proposals should be avoided to the extent possible. In a mega-dispute such as a nationwide doctors' strike, submitting a mediator's proposal was a rare exception to this rule.

The mediators' proposal was made under special circumstances and as part of our decision to end the mediation. In this particular context, the intended function of the mediators' proposal was to provide a single text in order to focus and set a framework for the negotiation.

I initially objected to the idea that we should announce our resignation after three weeks of mediation and provide the parties with a proposal. In retrospect, it was a very effective mediation tactic. In many ways it was a turning point, speeding up the intra-organizational negotiations, primarily as regards the no-strike arbitration model. Our mediators' proposal was a true single text. In the event, the general principles and the structure we recommended for the economic package were adopted. The proposed Public Commission and the no-strike arbitration model were later reduced to writing and became, after slight modifications, part of the final agreement.

The mediators' proposal also had some drawbacks. The parties kept trying to convince us to change the proposal. They failed to understand that once the proposal was out, they could change anything they wanted without our consent.

However, the document would turn out to be their agreement, and they chose not to draft a new version of the mediators' proposal. Second, when the content of our proposal was released to the press, against our will and our unequivocal instructions, it infuriated people who had opposed the mediation. They viewed the mediators' proposal as an advisory non-binding arbitration award. Since they equated the mediation with arbitration, the written document reinforced their misunderstanding about the mediation.

THE SIDE-TABLE MEDIATION

The mediation with the Interns' Association regarding the restraining order they had obtained in their suit against the Finance Ministry concerning work after on-duty shifts highlighted another benefit of mediation: the mediator's ability to redefine the boundaries of the negotiation table. It enabled the mediators to reach out and bring into the negotiation participants, including unofficial ones, who could not be brought in by the parties themselves. In the doctors' mediation, the mediators brought into the consensus-building process the Interns' Association, a group that was recognized neither by the IMA nor by the employers, but that was needed in order to effectuate the deal.

CONFIDENTIALITY

The subject of confidentiality has received much attention in the ADR and mediation literature.[13] Its importance is unquestionable. Nonetheless, as our experience proved, in mega-disputes it is unreasonable to expect that strict confidentiality will be maintained by all.

The ground rules for the mediation called for strict confidentiality and a media blackout. Only our spokesperson was authorized to release daily joint statements about the progress of the mediation. Due to her ceaseless efforts to detect potential violations and our repeated pleas to the parties, these ground rules were kept throughout the six weeks of mediation.

The picture changed as we moved from the inner circle of those actively involved in the process to the outer circle, which included the Prime Minister, the Finance Minister, the Minister of Health and other officials and public relations officers. It may well be that we did not do enough to explain how and why confidentiality and the media blackout were essential for the parties and for the mediation process. We might also have offered them the services of our spokesperson in this respect. Nevertheless, given the fact that these were high-level politicians over whom we had little influence or control and who had their own agendas, it would have been unrealistic to expect different results.

In conclusion, even in a high-profile mega-mediation it is possible to secure a high degree of confidentiality, at least as far as those who are actively involved in the negotiations are concerned. The problem is that negotiations in mega-disputes are never isolated from potential intervention by high-level officials, such as the Prime Minister, other Cabinet members and their staff. Our experience taught us that it was impractical to enforce, and probably unreasonable to expect, the same degree of confidentiality from these officials. Consequently, whenever mediators talk with high-level officials they need to continuously emphasize the importance of maintaining strict confidentiality. At the same time, the mediators need to be cognizant of their inability to ensure confidentiality entirely to protect the parties, as well as the mediation process itself, from the negative ramifications associated with the unavoidable cracks in the "shell of confidentiality."

THE ROLE OF OPTIMISM

It may sound naive. Nonetheless, the mediation of the doctors' strike proved once again that endless optimism, sometimes in the face of all logic, is probably a necessary personality trait of a mediator. In this case, our high level of optimism remained constant against all odds. It bonded the mediators and the participants, and carried the negotiations through several severe crises.

Throughout the mediation we expressed our endless optimism and our strong confidence in the parties' ability to quickly reach an agreement that would end the strike and serve the interests of the public and the doctors' community. It was surprising to see how, as negotiations progressed, our expressions of confidence, optimism and enthusiasm became part of the parties' own discourse. Finally, I believe that without our infusion of hope and optimism, the parties would have been unable to accept the basic ideas of the no-strike arbitration and the Public Commission and to make them the cornerstone of the settlement.

The mediation of the doctors' strike was an extreme case in which the mediators' optimism played a pivotal role and was responsible for much of the transformation in the parties' attitudes. This was the reason I titled my address in the signing ceremony "The Triumph of Optimism."

NOTES

1. Yael, my partner, my children Roy, Hila and Aya, and my law firm partners and staff deserve my gratitude for putting up with my long absences. Unfortunately Miki was unable to make such a commitment. He went abroad twice on business

trips. The second such was long and resulted in his missing the last full week of the mediation.

2. For me, one of these rare exceptions was the labor law class I was teaching at the university. It so happened that the Director was a student of mine. In days I was scheduled to teach the meetings took place in Herzliya and we would adjourn the mediation sessions and go to class.

3. The process also requires mediators to have endless stamina. Given the back-to-back private caucuses, the mediators had no time for rest. In addition, in prolonged marathon sessions such as the ones that characterized this mediation, one of the mediator's functions is to maintain the energy level of the meeting.

4. During the last week of the doctors' mediation, Miki was absent and Jonathan, one of our assistant mediators, had to conduct a workshop which had been planned months before and could not be postponed. The end result was that several important sessions were run by two member team only.

5. This forum was established quite early in the mediation in order to sort out the problems with the data. Towards the end of the mediation, this forum was running cost simulations and took responsibility for reducing the economic package to numbers and fine tuning.

6. See: Thomas A. Kochan, "A Theory of Multilateral Bargaining in City Government" 27 *Indus. & Lab. Rel. Rev.* 525 (1974).

7. By creating new value through interest-based creative solutions. See; Lax & Sebenius, *supra*, note 2, ch. 7.

8. See: Mironi, *supra*, note 2; Mironi, *supra*, note 3, ch. 10.

9. William L. Ury, Jeanne M. Brett & Stephen B. Goldberg, *Getting Disputes Resolved–Designing Systems to Cut Costs of Conflict* 41 (1989).

10. Raday, *Supra*, note 2, ch. 9.

11. For the impact of the lawyers' philosophical map on the negotiation process, see Leonard Riskin, "Mediation and Lawyers" 43 *Ohio. St. L. J.* 29 (1982).

12. The distinction between deal-making negotiation and settlement negotiation was developed recently in Robert H. Mnookin, Scott R. Peppet & Andrew S. Tulumello, *Beyond Winning: Negotiating to Create Value in Deals and Disputes* (2000).

13. Note, "Protecting Confidentiality in Mediation" 98 *Harv. L.Rev.* 441 (1984); Lawrence R. Freedman & Michael L. Prigoff, "Confidentiality in Mediation: The Need for Protection" 2 *Ohio St. J. Dis. Res.* 37 (1986); Henry J. Brown & Arthur L. Marriott, *ADR Principles and Practices* 2nd Ed. 473–478, 486–492 (1999).

Epilogue

The agreement ended the doctors' strike. At the same time, it marked the beginning of a new era in labor relations for doctors in the public health sector in Israel. The seeds of change that were planted during the mediation started to grow almost immediately.

Ten months after the agreement was signed, the Prime Minister appointed the Public Commission. The scope of the Public Commission's charter was broad. It was instructed to adopt a systemic approach and to recommend strategic changes in the public health care system and in doctors' working conditions. The parties to the agreement invested huge efforts and submitted voluminous studies and working papers to the Public Commission. In December 2002, more than two years after its appointment and following many hearings and long deliberations, the Public Commission issued its final report.

Our involvement as mediators did not end at the signing ceremony. I continued to work with the Prime Minister's Chief of Staff and the General Manager of the Ministry of Health to ascertain that the Interns' Association received a letter confirming the Government's intent to initiate legislative change, as it had promised before the agreement was signed. Miki and I were asked to address the Public Commission to explain the underlying rationale for the Public Commission itself and our view as to its mission. I was also asked to assist the lawyers representing the IMA and the Division to conclude their negotiations over the design of the arbitration procedures.

My impression has been that as a form of third-party intervention, mediation has not yet fully been embraced or even accepted even by all those who took an active part in the mediation process. This observation refers primarily to several public officials from the Finance Ministry.

There are probably many reasons for their negative view of the mediation experience, of which the following are worth mentioning: their resistance to the active role of the Prime Minister and his office during the mediation, the scars from the unpleasant debates with the mediators over data, the difficulty in accepting the Prime Minister's decision to submit future negotiation disputes to arbitration and blaming the mediation for it, and, last but not least, the unfortunate fact that they still confuse mediation with arbitration. Clearly, much educational work still needs to be done.

The negotiations under the new no-strike arbitration regime will probably start soon. It will be interesting to see whether, in addition to resolving the strike and placing the public health care system and its labor relations on a path of strategic change, the mediation process was successful in creating a new foundation for a more constructive, transformative and interest-based discourse.

Index